Knitting
THE EASY WAY

pil Publications International, Ltd.

Writer: Terry Kimbrough
Technical editor: Jean Lampe
Consultant: Barbara Albright
Illustrator: Joni Coniglio

Designers: Berroco, Inc.; Beth Brown-Reinsel; Lisa Daniels; Judy Dercum; Phyllis Fishberg; Laurie Gonyea; Charlene Hatfield; Darlene Hayes; Terry Kimbrough; Marilyn King; Amy Merritt; Needful Yarns Design Studio; Beth Walker O'Brien; Jessica Peterson; Lucie Sinkler; JoAnne Turcotte; Sharon Turner; Adrienne Welch

Photography: Silver Lining Digital, Inc.
Prop styling: Danita Cherney
Models: Ford Models, Inc./Alexandra Bussey; Silver Lining Digital, Inc./Skyla Washington; Stewart Talent/Conor Burke, Connor Burns, Michael Erickson, Liliana Favela, Erin Johnson, Anna Weith

Additional photography: Introduction © Deborah Van Kirk; front cover background and end sheets © M. Angelo/Corbis; title page photo © Siede/Preis
Contributing illustrator: Stephanie Carter/Stephanie Carter Illustration, Ltd. (yarn ball icon)
Wooden hat stand: Kim Carleton Graves/www.finehatstands.com (pages 141, 147, and 149)

Louis Weber, CEO
Publications International, Ltd.
7373 North Cicero Avenue
Lincolnwood, Illinois 60712

Manufactured in China.

8 7 6 5 4 3 2 1

ISBN: 1-4127-1270-X

Library of Congress Control Number: 2005927781

Contents

The Wonder of Knitting

Imagine...

the wonder of simple balls of yarn transformed, stitch by stitch, into beautiful, perfectly fitted sweaters or a treasured one-of-a-kind gift. Feel the satisfaction of finishing the last stitch and knowing that you've made your own creation, something that is uniquely yours.

Join the thousands of women and men—teenagers, children, young mothers, seniors, celebrities—who are discovering their passion for knitting. All it takes to get started is a ball of yarn, a pair of knitting needles, our helpful guidebook, and a little practice. The fashionable sweaters, luxurious throws, adorable children's clothing, fabulous accessories, and special gifts presented in the following pages will inspire you. The clearly written, well-illustrated instructions will ensure your success. No doubt you'll be planning your next project before the first is even finished!

So you've never knit before? There's no reason to feel intimidated. Remember when you got your first big box of crayons? Can you recall the satisfaction and joy you felt as you chose each color? You'd make colorful rainbows, rows of flowers, and big yellow suns. Or you'd color in your favorite coloring book, choosing just the right shade. Were you told all those pesky rules about coloring within the lines? Promise yourself that when you take out your yarn and needles it will be all about the joy of creation, with no pressure to measure up to anyone's idea of perfection—not even your own.

Before you know it, you'll be knitting like a pro. Celebrate each stitch on your journey—beginning with the very first one.

Getting Started

Knitting is as simple as pulling one loop through another. The action will feel awkward at first, but with a little practice, knitting will become very natural. You won't even have to think about what you're doing! Read on—you'll be hooked in no time.

What Do I Need?

Begin by purchasing a pair of straight knitting needles, size 8 or 9. Aluminum needles are inexpensive, and most novice knitters start with this type. Read on to learn more about knitting needles. Next, you need some yarn. Purchase a ball or two of light-color, *smooth* worsted weight wool yarn. **Worsted weight** is a yarn thickness (see page 6). Ask the store personnel for worsted weight yarn, or check the yarn label to determine if it is worsted weight. Choose wool to start your practice pieces because it's easy to work with and very elastic, and choose a light color to help you better "see" the stitches and follow the yarn path. The simple items needed for your first knitting steps are available in all knitting shops or craft stores. Department stores may also carry a number of items for knitting and crochet. We'll assume you have scissors and a tape measure, and for the beginning steps, this is all you'll need to get started. The following pages explain needles, yarn, and accessories in greater detail. For more information on knitting stitches, flip to page 9.

Needles

Needles are available in a wide variety of materials: aluminum, plastic, and other fabricated substances, along with natural woods. You can make your own needles out of dowels sharpened on one end. Or you can buy rare antique, sterling silver, or gold-plated needles, or even needles with the ends adorned with precious gems. Whichever you choose, just know they all knit the same, and all can get lost in the cushions of the couch.

Novice knitters may prefer to use needles of bamboo or wood because the stitches are less likely to slide off. These materials help grip the stitches. With experience, you'll find a type or brand of knitting needle that becomes your favorite. To begin, it's a good idea to buy an inexpensive pair that appeals to you, and start from there.

Needles come in a range of sizes, from a very tiny size 0 (you don't want to start with these!) all the way up to size 50 (you'll only use these in rare instances for specialty projects). Knitting patterns include a *suggested* needle size. You won't know the actual size you need to work the pattern until after you make your gauge swatch. (See Gauge, page 16.)

There are three styles of knitting needles: straight (single-point), circular, and double-point needles. The most common style is **straight, single-point.** These needles are sold in pairs and are available in both 10- and 14-inch lengths. They have a knob on the end opposite the point to prevent stitches from slipping off. The needle size is sometimes stamped on the knob or on the needle shank. Straight needles are best suited to working back and forth in rows to make a flat piece of knitting.

To avoid sewing seams, you can work in rounds using **circular** needles. Circular needles consist of two short needles connected by a thin, plastic cable. When choosing circular needles, look at the place where the

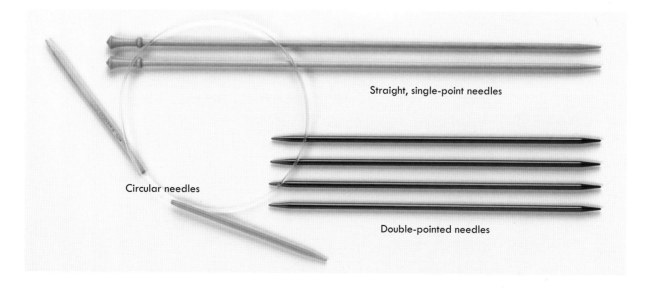

Straight, single-point needles

Circular needles

Double-pointed needles

cable connects to the needle. It should be smooth so stitches glide easily from cable to needle. Circular needles are available in most ordinary sizes, with cable lengths of 16, 20, 24, 29, and 36 inches. Use a length that comfortably holds the number of stitches you are using. Circular needles are used for seamless, knit-in-the-round items, but they can be used to knit flat pieces as well.

The third type is **double-pointed** needles. These short needles have an identical point on each end, and either end is used to knit. Double-pointed needles are usually sold in sets of 4 or 5 and are available in lengths from 6 to 8 inches. Shorter lengths are available for making socks or gloves. This type of needle is best used for knitting in the round or for making I-cords or other small, flat items made with few stitches.

Yarn

The only thing more fun than finishing the last stitch of a project is choosing the yarn you'll use for the next one. There is a huge selection of yarns and colors available, and choosing one can be the most difficult part of your project. Arm yourself with the following information, and you'll be sure to choose yarn that you love and is perfect for your project.

Once you find a pattern you like, read the materials list carefully. It tells you everything you need to know about the yarn you'll be using. Most patterns specify the exact brand and color used, which makes shopping much easier. Check with your local yarn shop to see if they carry that yarn, and in what colors. If they don't, they should be able to suggest an alternative. Or search for the yarn at one of the many online shops.

When substituting yarn, always choose a yarn from within the same weight category, that is a similar fiber, and has a similar gauge (see Gauge, page 16). Once you know these three things, you can consider other brands of yarn to substitute.

The pattern tells you what weight of yarn to use. Yarn weight falls into several categories. The basic five are: fingering, sport, DK, worsted, and bulky. **Fingering,** or **baby,** weight yarn is very fine. It's often used for socks, lacework, and baby clothes. **Sport** weight yarn is heavier than fingering weight and can be used for almost anything, including afghans, baby items, crafts, and sweaters. **DK** weight stands for double knit and is thicker than sport weight. It is pri-

marily a European yarn weight, though several American companies are now importing it under their own company name. **Worsted** weight is the most commonly used yarn. It's used for sweaters, afghans, pillows, and many other items. It works up quickly and is a good weight for new knitters. **Bulky,** or **chunky,** weight yarn is used for rugs, coats, and heavy sweaters. It is thick and heavy and works up very quickly on extra-large needles.

Within each of these categories are all sorts of yarn made from many different **fibers.** The fiber most often associated with knitting is **wool.** Wool is a beautiful, durable yarn that is a pleasure to work with and holds its shape well. Check the fabric care symbols on the label carefully—many wools aren't machine washable. Before you choose wool, make sure you're willing to care for it properly. **Cotton** yarns are very popular because they make a cool and comfortable product. Cotton is usually labeled as hand-wash only. **Blends** are any imaginable combination of fibers, including natural and synthetic. While most knitters prefer natural fibers, synthetics have their advantages. They are often inexpensive, readily available, offer a wide

Fingering, or baby, weight yarn

Sport weight yarn

DK weight yarn

Worsted weight yarn

Bulky, or chunky, weight yarn

Yarn ball

Skein

Hank

any difference when comparing two different dye lots in the store, but after completing a project, you'll realize just how "off" two balls of "Off-White" can be. The probability of buying or finding matching dye lots months later is unlikely. Check each dye lot number, and buy all the yarn you'll need *before* you start your project. You'll be very glad you did.

Additional Supplies, Tools, and Accessories

Needles and yarn will get you started, but as your knitting skills progress, you'll want to acquire the following:

Scissors Any sharp, pointed scissors will do. Springs in the handles are also great time-savers, since you simply squeeze to clip the yarn.

Tape measure or ruler For the most accurate measurements, use a hard ruler. Use a yardstick for larger

color selection, and are easy to care for. Choose a yarn that's right for your pattern and based on your personal taste. A good tip is to buy one ball or skein (called the *ball* from here on) of the yarn you want to use before starting the project. Knit up a large swatch in the stitch pattern, and wash or dry-clean it in the same manner you'll use for your finished project. You'll learn several things from this experiment: your gauge, if you like working with the yarn, if the yarn shrinks or stretches after cleaning, and, most important, if the dye runs.

The next question is "How much yarn do I buy?" That information is found in the pattern materials list and on the yarn label. If you buy the brand the pattern calls for, simply check to see how many balls are needed for the size you're making. When substituting yarns, first determine if the new yarn ball has the same number of yards (meters) as the pattern yarn. (See Yards vs. Meters, page 38.) Check the yarn label to see how many yards or meters the ball contains, and divide this number into the total yardage needed to determine how many balls you need. Round this number up to the nearest ball to make sure you'll have enough yarn.

Before purchasing, check the **dye lot** number on every ball of yarn you've selected. Yarn is dyed in huge lots, or batches. When distributed to retail stores, dye lots are often mixed together. You may not be able to see

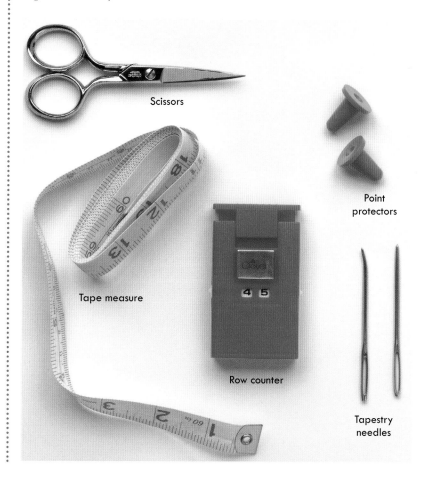

Scissors

Point protectors

Tape measure

Row counter

Tapestry needles

items. If using a tape measure, buy a new one. Old tape measures tend to stretch and lose their accuracy.

Tapestry needles Tapestry needles (also called yarn needles) are oversize sewing needles used for sewing seams and weaving in yarn tails. A tapestry needle has a large eye, suitable for threading yarns. It's a good idea to have both blunt and sharp needles. The blunt style weaves seams without snagging stitches, and the sharp needle will slide through stitches when weaving yarn tails.

Point protectors Point protectors are rubber tips that fit over the knitting needle tips to prevent stitches falling off. They also keep the sharp needle points from jabbing something. Protectors come in several sizes, and you'll need a few to fit various needles.

Row counter This gadget helps keep track of the number of rows worked. Some slip onto the needles and are turned after each row; others sit by your side and are clicked after each row. Or, in place of a purchased counter, paper and pencil also work.

More Handy Things

It's likely you'll eventually want to add the following tools to your knitting bag.

Bobbins Bobbins are usually made of plastic and hold small amounts of yarn cut from the main ball. Knitters use bobbins for working intarsia knitting (patterns with a lot of color changes). The yarn is wrapped around the bobbin and then pulled through one end and joined to the knitting at the appropriate place.

Cable needles These short needles are used when crossing cable stitches. There are three basic types: a short, straight double-pointed needle; a double-pointed needle with a dip in the center (to hold the stitches); and a U-shaped needle with one leg longer than the other. The style you choose is a matter of preference.

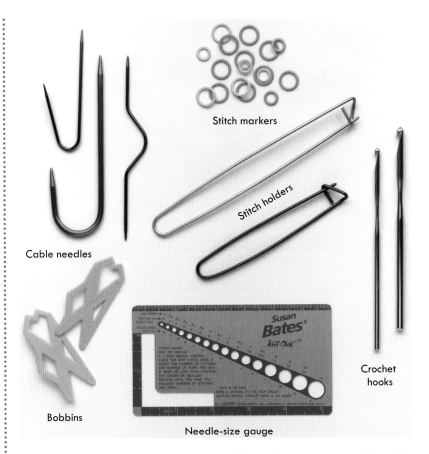

Cable needles

Stitch markers

Stitch holders

Bobbins

Needle-size gauge

Crochet hooks

Cable needles are available in different diameters. Choose one slightly smaller than your project needles. You only need one cable needle for a specific project because it is used only once for each cable twist.

Crochet hooks These hooks have many uses: picking up stitches, rethreading dropped stitches (see Dropped Stitches, page 20), closing seams, or working crocheted edgings around knitted pieces (see Crochet, page 25). Some cast-on methods use a crochet hook.

Needle-size gauge This tool features a window that allows you to measure stitch and row gauge at the same time. Some styles also have holes with which to measure basic needle sizes.

Stitch holder A stitch holder holds stitches off the needle until you need them. There are several types available, including one that works like a safety pin. Many knitters use a length

of smooth cotton yarn and thread it through the stitches, tying the ends into an overhand knot to prevent the stitches from slipping off.

Stitch markers These little tools help mark pattern sections, increases or decreases, or the beginning of a round in circular knitting. Markers are slipped onto your needle or are attached to the work through a stitch. When casting on many stitches, place a marker after every 20th stitch, and speedily count across the row in sections of 20 stitches. To hold your place in a pattern, slip the marker from left to right needle on every row. Markers come in assorted sizes; use the size closest to your needle size. Using one that is too large may stretch and distort your stitches.

Little extras Other useful things to keep in your bag are knitter's coilless pins, safety pins, a small notebook and pen or pencil, rustproof T-pins for blocking, sticky notes for mark-

Making a Slipknot

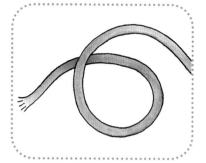

Fig. 1a

Fig. 1b

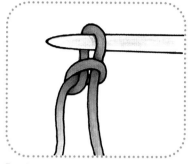

Fig. 1c

ing your place in patterns or taking notes, an emery board to smooth a rough edge on a needle, and a travel pack of tissues.

It's Time to Knit!

Take out a ball of yarn and a pair of needles, and get that first stitch on your needle!

Casting On (CO)

The cast-on row is the foundation row of knitting. There are many ways to cast on stitches. One method may be faster or easier for you or may work better for certain techniques, such as buttonholes. Try each of the cast-on methods below, and start with the one that appeals to you most. **Note:** The cast-on should be as elastic as the body of your knitting. If needed, the cast-on may be worked using a needle two or three sizes larger than your gauge needle. Knit the stitches onto the smaller needle as you knit the first row.

Making a Slipknot The first stitch on your needle for most cast-on methods is a **slipknot**.

Step 1: Hold the yarn in your left hand about 8 inches from the end. With your right hand, make a circle with the yarn (*fig. 1a*). If it's helpful, hold the circle together between your index finger and thumb to prevent it from slipping away.

Step 2: With the working yarn behind the circle, insert the knitting needle through the circle from front

to back and catch the working yarn, pulling it through the circle and forming a loop (*fig. 1b*).

Step 3: With the new loop on the needle in your right hand, gently pull both yarns (the tail and the working yarn attached to the ball) beneath the needle, then pull on the working yarn to tighten the new loop so that it fits snugly around the needle (*fig. 1c*).

Cable Cast-on This cast-on is especially good when you need a firm edge. Work loosely, without pulling the stitches too tight.

Cable Cast-on

Fig. 2a

Fig. 2b

Fig. 2c

Fig. 2d

Step 1: In your left hand, hold the needle with the slipknot and hold the working yarn in your right hand. Insert the right needle through the slipknot from front to back (*fig. 2a*).

Step 2: Wrap the yarn around the right needle from back to front and pull up a loop, creating a new stitch on the right needle. Insert the left needle tip into the new stitch (*fig. 2b*), and slip it onto the left needle. There are now 2 stitches on the left needle (*fig. 2c*). **Note:** To prevent the cast-on edge from becoming too tight, insert the right needle from front to

The Knitty-Gritty

Knit Loops and Purl Loops

Before you venture any further, look at these six illustrations. They will help you understand many things about knitting, so study them well and plan to return to this page often. When a cast-on or stitch pattern specifies working into the **front loop** or **back loop**, simply match the instruction to the illustration to see exactly which part of the stitch is being described.

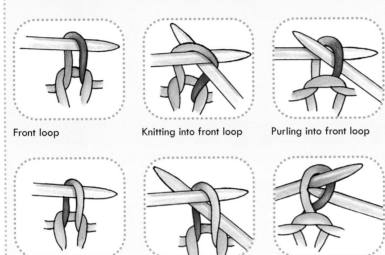

Front loop

Knitting into front loop

Purling into front loop

Back loop

Knitting into back loop

Purling into back loop

back between the 2 stitches on the left needle before tightening the yarn. Gently pull the working yarn to snug up the stitch.

Step 3: With the right needle in position between the 2 stitches on the left needle, wrap the yarn around the right needle as shown *(fig. 2c)*, and pull through a new loop.

Step 4: Using the tip of the left needle, slip the new stitch from the right needle as before *(fig. 2d)*, and slip the right needle out of the stitch.

Repeat steps 3 and 4 to cast on additional stitches. End with step 4 to complete the last cast-on stitch.

Long Tail (or Slingshot) Cast-on The benefits of this cast-on method are that it's quick to do and makes an elastic edge. Both working yarn and tail are used.

The tail length should be roughly three times the width of your desired cast-on, or about 1 inch (2.5cm) per stitch for worsted weight yarn, plus several inches extra for the yarn tail

allowance to weave in later. If you underestimate the length of yarn tail needed, pull out the work, add more yarn to the length, and begin again. Or, begin the cast-on using two balls of the same yarn: One serves as the "tail," and the other is the working yarn. Tie the ends together in an overhand knot, leaving about a 6-inch (15cm) tail, and then make the slipknot as usual and begin the cast-on. When the cast-on is completed, cut one of the yarns, leaving about 6 inches (15cm), and begin to work with the other. When the garment is finished, untie the overhand knot and weave in the loose ends.

Step 1: Place the slipknot onto the needle held in your right hand, with the yarn tail in front (closest to you) and the working yarn (attached to the ball) behind the needle. Pull the working yarn taut over the left forefinger, and wrap the yarn tail around your thumb from front to back. Secure both the working yarn and the tail between the remaining 3 fingers of your left hand and the palm. Place the forefinger of your right hand on top of the slipknot to hold it in place *(fig. 3a)*.

Step 2: Insert the needle under the yarn in front of your thumb, working from front to back and pulling the yarn slightly upward *(fig. 3b)*. Insert the needle over the yarn on your forefinger, moving from top to bottom so the working yarn lies on top of the needle to form the new stitch *(fig. 3b)*.

Long Tail (or Slingshot) Cast-on

Fig. 3a

Fig. 3b

Fig. 3c

Simple Cast-on (Backward Loop Cast-on)

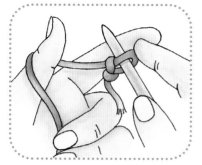

Fig. 4a

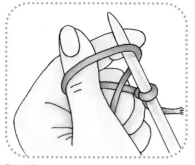

Fig. 4b

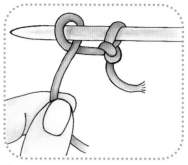

Fig. 4c

Step 3: Pull the needle toward you through the loop on your thumb as you remove your thumb from the loop *(fig. 3c)*. At the same time, pull down on both pieces of yarn, tightening the stitch by pulling on the tail, keeping the stitch firm and even but still loose enough to slide easily.

Repeat steps to cast on additional stitches.

Simple Cast-on (Backward Loop Cast-on) This cast-on is probably the easiest to learn, but it doesn't have a neat edge like other cast-ons. Use it when working a few cast-on stitches or on buttonholes. This cast-on tends to grow longer and become less manageable as you work the first row of knitting, and the cast-on stitches tighten, making it difficult to insert the needle.

Step 1: Place the slipknot (page 9), on an empty needle with the yarn tail in back and the working yarn in front. Hold this needle with the slipknot in your right hand.

Step 2: With working yarn in your left hand, wrap the working yarn over your thumb from front to back, and grasp it with your remaining fingers to tension *(fig. 4a)*.

Step 3: Insert the needle under the yarn looped around your thumb, working from bottom to top *(fig. 4b)*. Pull up on the needle a little as you slide the yarn off your thumb and onto the needle.

Step 4: Gently pull on the working yarn to tighten the new stitch on the needle *(fig. 4c)*.

Repeat steps 2–4 to cast on as many stitches as desired. End with step 4.

Knitted Cast-on This cast-on is easy to work and is very similar to the cable cast-on (page 9). The difference between the cable cast-on and the knitted cast-on occurs after the first stitch is made.

Step 1: Place the slipknot on an empty needle and hold in your left hand, with the working yarn in your right hand. Insert the right needle through the slipknot from front to back *(see fig. 2a, page 9)*.

Step 2: Wrap the yarn around the right needle from back to front, and pull up a loop, creating a new stitch on the right needle. Insert the left needle tip into the new stitch *(see fig. 2b, page 9)*. Both needles remain in the new stitch.

Repeat step 2 for each new stitch until all cast-on stitches are made.

Withdraw the right needle after the last stitch is made. Although both needles remain in the new loop at all times, the stitches collect on the left needle only.

The Stitches

Knitting has two basic stitches: the knit stitch and the purl stitch. After mastering these stitches, you'll be able to create many stitch patterns. Knitting is enjoyed and practiced all over the world, but not everyone knits in the same style. There is no right or wrong style of knitting. This book presents two of the more common knitting methods used in America: the American-English method, with the yarn held in the right hand, and the Continental method, with the yarn held in the left hand.

Holding the Yarn

Experiment with the way you hold the yarn. Weave the yarn through your fingers as shown below, or try

American-English method

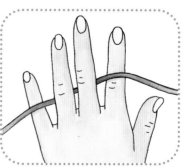

Continental method

other ways until you find a method that works for you and feels comfortable. The ability to tension the yarn as it flows through your fingers while knitting allows you to maintain your gauge and work neat, even stitches. It's also less tiring on the hands.

Knit Stitch (k)

The knit stitch is the most common and versatile stitch of all. It is smooth on one side and bumpy on the other. The smooth side is generally used as the right side of the work—the side that faces out. The working yarn is always held behind the needle when making the knit stitch. In other words, the knit fabric and the needle will always be between you and the working yarn. When working flat, back and forth knitting, knitting every row creates **garter stitch** (see page 15).

Knit Stitch American-English Method

Step 1: Hold the needle with the cast-on stitches in your left hand. The working yarn is already attached to the stitch closest to the needle tip. Hold the empty needle in your right hand; take hold of the working yarn with your right hand, and hold it behind the right needle. Insert the empty needle from front to back through the first stitch on the left needle *(fig. 5a)*. The right needle is **underneath** the left needle.
Step 2: Bring your right hand and forefinger toward the tip of the right needle (the yarn is underneath the right needle). Wrap the yarn around the right needle from back to front *(fig. 5b)*. Be careful not to wrap it around the left needle, too.
Step 3: Keeping the yarn firmly tensioned in your right hand, bring the right needle toward you, pulling a new loop through the old stitch *(fig. 5c)*.
Step 4: With the new stitch on the right needle, slip the old stitch off

Knit Stitch American-English Method

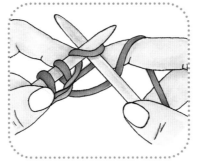
Fig. 5a

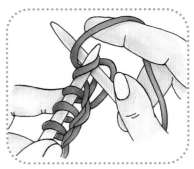
Fig. 5b

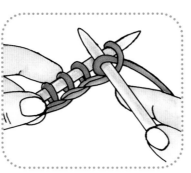
Fig. 5c

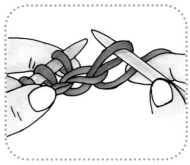
Fig. 5d

the left needle *(fig. 5d)*. Unlike the cast-on, the new knit stitches are held on the right needle.

You have just knit your first stitch, American-English style. Repeat until all the cast-on stitches have been knit and are on the needle held in the right hand. Jump ahead to Knitting the Next Row, or cast on another 20 stitches and try the knit stitch, Continental style.

Knit Stitch, Continental Method

As in the American-English method, the yarn is always held behind the work when making the knit stitch.
Step 1: Hold the working yarn and the needle with the cast-on stitches in your left hand and the empty needle in your right hand. Insert the empty needle into the first stitch on the left needle, from front to back *(fig. 6a)*. The right needle is under the left needle.
Step 2: Holding the yarn in your left hand, over the left forefinger and behind both needles, bring the yarn

over the right needle from left to right as shown *(fig. 6b)*. Be careful not to wrap it around the left needle.
Step 3: Keeping the yarn firmly in your hand, pull the right needle and the yarn loop toward you, through the cast-on stitch *(fig. 6c)*.
Step 4: With the new stitch on the right needle, slip the old stitch off the left needle *(fig. 6d)*. Unlike the cast-on stitches, the new knit stitches are held on the right needle.

You have just knit your first stitch, Continental style. Repeat until all the cast-on stitches have been knit.

Knitting the Next Row, Either Style

The second and all subsequent knit rows are worked the same as the first: Knit each stitch on the needle in the left hand.
Step 1: When you have knit all the stitches from the left needle, turn the work, switching the needle with all the stitches on it from your right hand to your left.

Knit Stitch, Continental Method

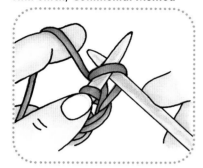

Fig. 6a

Fig. 6b

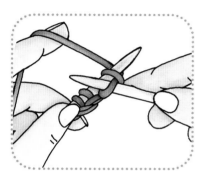

Fig. 6c

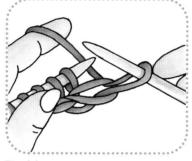

Fig. 6d

Step 2: The working yarn is attached to the stitch closest to the needle tip. Insert the right needle into the first stitch and repeat the knitting steps across the first row, working into each of the stitches of the previous row instead of into the cast-on stitches.

Note: When beginning each new row, make sure the working yarn is *beneath* the needle holding the stitches and is not wrapped over the needle. If the working yarn is pulled upward, the first stitch will appear as two stitches, with both stitch loops appearing in front of the needle. If you knit both loops as single stitches, you'll increase the number of stitches on your needle. Remember, the front loop of each stitch should be in front of the needle and the back loop behind the needle (see Knit Loops and Purl Loops, page 10).

As soon as you feel comfortable making the knit stitch, you can try the easier projects in the book (they are noted by an icon of one ball of yarn; projects of increasing complexity are marked with two or three balls of yarn). To finish these projects, you'll also need to practice binding off (see

page 14). For most projects, you'll also need to know the purl stitch.

Purl Stitch (p)

The purl stitch is the reverse of the knit stitch. The yarn is always held in *front* of the work when making the purl stitch. As you work this stitch, the bumpy side faces you and the side behind the needle is now the smooth side. When working flat, back and forth knitting, purling every row creates **garter stitch,** just the same as knitting every row. Alternating rows of knit and purl makes **stockinette stitch,** in which the knit side is the right side and the purl side is the wrong side (see page 15). The purl side of stockinette stitch is called **reverse stockinette stitch,** which uses the purl side as the right side and the knit side as the wrong side.

Purl Stitch, American-English Method

Step 1: Hold the working yarn and the empty needle in your right hand and the needle with the cast-on stitches in your left hand. With the working yarn held in front of your work, insert the empty needle from right to left through the front loop of the first stitch *(fig. 7a).* The right needle is in front of the left needle.

Step 2: Bring the yarn in your right hand toward the tip of the right needle. Carry the yarn between the needles, and wrap it around the right needle from front to back, ending in front *(fig. 7b).* Be careful not to wrap it around the left needle.

Purl Stitch, American-English Method

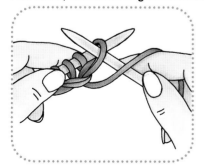

Fig. 7a

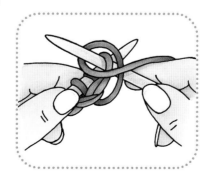

Fig. 7b

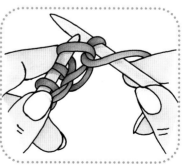

Fig. 7c

Purl Stitch, Continental Method

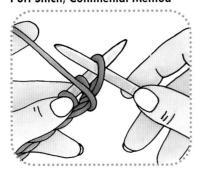

Fig. 8a

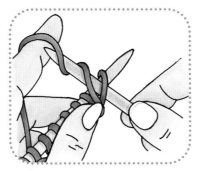

Fig. 8b

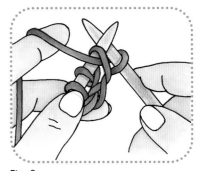

Fig. 8c

Step 3: Keeping the working yarn firmly in your right hand, use the right needle to pull up a loop, moving backward and away from you through the stitch on the left needle *(fig. 7c)*. With the new stitch on the right needle, slip the old stitch off the left needle.

Repeat for each new stitch.

Purl Stitch, Continental Method
Step 1: Hold the working yarn and the cast-on stitches in your left hand and the empty needle in your right hand. With the yarn held in front of your work, insert the empty needle from right to left through the front loop of the first stitch on the left needle *(fig. 8a)*. The right needle is in front of the left needle.
Step 2: Wrap the yarn around the right needle from front to back, ending in the front *(fig. 8b)*.
Step 3: Keeping the yarn firmly in your left hand, use the right needle to pull a loop through the old stitch on the left needle, moving backward

and away from you *(fig. 8c)*. With the new stitch on the right needle, slip the old stitch off the left needle.

Repeat for each new stitch.

Purling the Next Row
The second and subsequent purl rows are worked the same as the first. Purl each stitch on the needle in the left hand.
Step 1: When you have purled all the stitches from the left needle, turn the work, switching the needle with all the stitches from right hand to left.
Step 2: The working yarn is attached to the stitch closest to the needle tip and held in front of the work. Insert the right needle into the first stitch with the yarn held in front of the stitches, and repeat the steps of the first row, working into each of the stitches in the previous row instead of the cast-on stitches.

Binding Off (BO)
This technique finishes the last row and secures the stitches so the nee-

dles can be removed. You will often see the phrase "bind off in pattern." This means work the last row of stitches as instructed, and bind off as you work. It sounds tricky, but it's not. The illustrations here show a knit row for the bind-off, but you'll want to practice the technique on both knit and purl rows.
Step 1: Hold the needle with stitches in your left hand and the empty needle in your right hand. Hold the yarn in position for the knit stitch, behind your work.
Step 2: Knit the first 2 stitches.
Step 3: Insert the left needle from left to right into the front loop of the first stitch on the right needle *(fig. 9a)*. **Note:** This is the stitch farther from the right needle tip.
Step 4: Use the left needle to pull this stitch over the second stitch and drop it off the right needle. One stitch bound off; the second stitch remains on the right needle *(fig. 9b)*.
Step 5: Knit the next stitch.

Binding Off

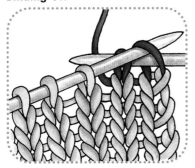

Fig. 9a

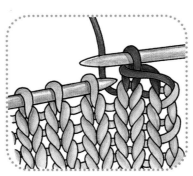

Fig. 9b

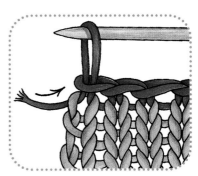

Fig. 9c

Garter Stitch

Fig. 10

Stockinette Stitch (knit side)

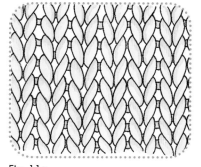

Fig. 11a

Reverse Stockinette Stitch (purl side)

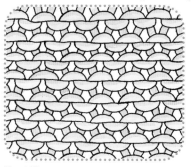

Fig. 11b

Step 6: Repeat steps 3–5 until you have bound off all stitches from the left needle and 1 stitch remains on the right needle. Cut the yarn about 4 inches from the stitch, and pull the yarn tail through the last stitch *(fig. 9c)*. Remove the needle and pull the yarn tail to tighten.

Many new knitters bind off too tightly. The bound-off edge should be as elastic as the rest of the knitting. If necessary, use a larger needle size to work the stitches in your bind-off row.

Basic Stitch Patterns

There are many ways to combine stitches to create different patterns, but the basis of every pattern is the knit stitch and the purl stitch.

Garter Stitch (g st)

Knit every row in flat knitting, and you have garter stitch *(fig. 10)*. It's a great stitch pattern for new knitters because it uses only one simple stitch. Because garter stitch lays flat without curling, it's often used at the beginning and ends of rows to create flat, non-curling edges. *Note:* If you knit in the round, on circular or double-pointed needles, you'll create stockinette stitch instead of garter stitch.

Stockinette Stitch (St st)

This is the most commonly used stitch pattern. Simply knit one row, purl the next, and repeat to produce this pattern. Stockinette stitch will

curl at the edges when not stabilized with other, non-curling, stitch patterns, such as garter stitch. Because of that, border stitch patterns are usually added to the lower and upper edges, and the side edges are sewn into the seam. To obtain an accurate measurement, you can block it (see Washing and Blocking, page 27) to keep it flat temporarily.

The knit side (the smooth side) is called stockinette stitch *(fig. 11a)*, and the purl side (or bumpy side) is called reverse stockinette stitch *(fig. 11b)*. Reverse stockinette stitch is often used as a background for cable patterns.

Ribbing (rib)

You'll recognize ribbing as the stitch found at the cuffs and hems of sweaters. It is a very elastic pattern and knits up narrower than stockinette stitch on the same size needles. There are many ways of making ribbing, but the most common are the **single rib** *(fig. 12a)* and the

double rib *(fig. 12b)*. The single rib is made by alternating one knit stitch with one purl stitch (abbreviated as k1,p1). The double rib is more elastic than the single rib and is made by alternating two knit stitches with two purl stitches (abbreviated k2,p2).

The most important thing to remember when making ribbing is that the yarn must be brought *between* the needles to the back of the work for the knit stitches and brought *between* the needles to the front of the work for the purl stitches. Sometimes new knitters finish a row and discover extra stitches, or they may find a hole in their ribbing several rows later. Knitting with the yarn in front or purling with the yarn in back is generally the cause. If you create a little mix-up with your stitches, remember that such things are easily corrected (see How to Correct Mistakes, page 20).

Ribbing is very easy once you have learned to recognize knit and purl stitches. Instead of counting

Ribbing

Fig. 12a

Fig. 12b

Gauge Swatch

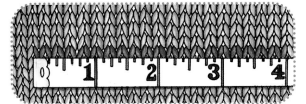

Fig. 13a

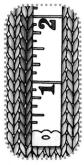

Fig. 13b

stitches, you simply knit the knits and purl the purls.

Is That All There Is to It?

You are now a knitter! Practice these basic stitches until you feel comfortable with them, and remember to refer back to the instructions if you get confused. Before you know it, you'll be making these stitches without needing to think about what your hands are doing.

You can use the simple knit and purl stitches to make many wonderful things. But don't stop there! If you keep challenging yourself to try new patterns and learn new techniques, knitting will continue to be an exciting adventure.

Gauge

The word **gauge** (or **tension**) refers to how many stitches (or rows) there are in an inch of knitting using a specific yarn and needle size. The resulting numbers are used to determine how many stitches and rows it will take to achieve a desired size. Remember, the needle size listed in the pattern is the size the designer used to obtain the listed gauge. Two knitters using the same materials may end up with different gauges. A difference of only half a stitch per inch could make a discrepancy of several inches in the size of the finished project. Take time to make a gauge swatch before starting your project—you'll be glad you did. It may be necessary to make several

attempts before you achieve the correct gauge.

How to Knit a Gauge Swatch Use the main needle size listed in the pattern. Cast on about 6 inches worth of stitches, using the stitch gauge given in the pattern to determine the number to cast on. Work the main pattern until the swatch measures 4 inches in length; bind off all stitches. Lay the swatch on a flat, hard surface. Measure, then count 4 inches worth of stitches across the swatch *(fig. 13a)*. Divide this number by 4 to get the number of stitches per inch. Repeat the process a few times in different areas to confirm the count. To measure the rows, center the measuring tape or ruler lengthwise on the swatch, and count the number of rows over 2 inches *(fig. 13b)*, or 4 inches if the pattern is very large vertically. Divide the total by 2 (or 4, if using that number) to determine the number of rows per inch. ***Note:*** Knit stitches are wider than they are tall. However, in stitch patterns such as stockinette stitch, you'll normally have *more* rows per inch than stitches per inch.

Compare your gauge with the pattern gauge. If your gauge swatch has **more stitches per inch** than the pattern gauge, this means your stitches are *smaller* than the pattern gauge, and you'll need to try **larger size needles** until your swatch stitches are the same size as the required gauge. If your swatch has

fewer stitches per inch than the pattern gauge, your stitches are *larger* than the pattern gauge, and you'll need to try **smaller size needles** to obtain the pattern gauge. Be exact in your measurements, and knit as many swatches as you need to, changing needle sizes until you find the size that allows you to obtain the correct gauge.

Knitting in the Round

To avoid sewing seams, you can work in rounds using **circular** needles or **double-pointed** needles.

Circular Needles To work in rounds, cast your stitches on one end of the needle the same as you would on a straight needle. Check to make sure that the cast-on lays flat and smooth and is not twisted. Add a stitch marker *(see page 8)* to the end of the needle to mark the beginning of the round *(fig. 14a),* and work the first round according to your pattern instructions.

Double-Pointed Needles Evenly distribute your cast-on over three or four needles, keeping one needle out to knit with. Make sure the cast-on lays flat and smooth and no stitches are twisted. If you'd like, add a stitch marker to the first needle to mark the beginning of the round. (It's easy for a stitch marker to fall off the double-pointed needle, however, so be careful.) The needles either form a triangle (if you cast on to three needles) *(fig. 14b)* or a square (if you cast on to four needles). With the empty needle, knit all stitches on the first needle. When that needle is empty, use it to knit the stitches on the next needle. Continue to knit the stitches from each double-point onto an empty needle, working the stitches as instructed in the pattern.

Slip Stitch (sl st)

Sometimes instructions tell you to **slip a stitch**. This means you'll move a stitch to the right needle

Knitting in the Round

Fig. 14a

without knitting or purling. The instructions may indicate whether to slip it as if to knit or purl. If told to slip a stitch, with no further reference, then slip as if to purl. **To slip as if to knit** *(fig. 15a)*, keep the yarn behind your work and insert the right needle into the next stitch on the left needle as if to knit it. However, instead of wrapping the yarn around the needle, simply slide the stitch off the left needle and onto the right. **To slip as if to purl with yarn in back** *(fig. 15b)*, with the knit side facing you, insert the right needle tip into the next stitch on the left needle as if to purl, and slide the stitch onto the right needle. **To slip as if to purl with yarn in front** *(fig. 15c)*, with purl side facing you, slip the stitch as if to purl. When a stitch is slipped using either of these

Fig. 14b

methods, the strand will not show on the knit side of the work. However, some stitch patterns reverse the normal process, so always follow instructions carefully.

Why does it make a difference how stitches are slipped? When stitches are slipped as if to purl, they are transferred onto the right needle untwisted, which means the front stitch loop remains in front of the needle. When slipped as if to knit, they are transferred in a twisted position. In other words, the back loop of the stitch is now in front. Some pattern stitches require this; others don't.

A rule of thumb about slipping stitches: Always slip as if to purl unless the pattern instructions specify otherwise. An exception to this rule is that you'll always slip as if to knit when the stitch is part of a decrease method. A stitch that's part of a decrease is transferred to the right needle as if to knit, in the

twisted position, because it will later become untwisted when the decrease is complete.

Increases (inc)

Increases are used to shape your knitting and to create lace patterns. There are many ways to make an increase; we've listed a few standard methods. Many pattern instructions specify which type of increase to use; others do not. It's important to learn how each increase affects the appearance of your work, so you can use the appropriate method. Make small knit swatches and practice each increase method listed here. Label them, and keep them for future reference. Avoid making increases and decreases in the edge stitches, because they affect the ability to make a smooth seam when finishing. Make increases or decreases at least one stitch in from the edge stitches.

Yarn Over (yo) A **yarn over** is the basis of most lace patterns and is very simple to make. In fact, many new knitters make yarn overs completely by accident (but in those cases it's called a hole, not lace). When moving the yarn from the front or the back of your work, you would normally be very careful to put the yarn between the needles and not over it (which would create an extra loop on the needle). To make a yarn over when knitting, bring the yarn to the front of the work and then knit the following stitches as

Slip Stitch

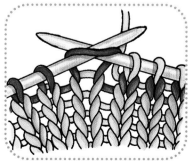

Fig. 15a

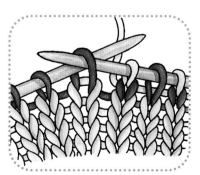

Fig. 15b

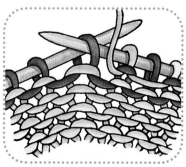

Fig. 15c

instructed *(fig. 16a)*. On the next row, work into the front loop of this strand (yarn over) as you would any other stitch, transferring it from the left needle after it is knitted.

Knit 1 in the Front and Back Loops (k1f&b)/Bar Increase This is one of the most visible increases in stockinette stitch—it leaves a little bump that looks like a purl stitch. Use it decoratively, or use it when the purl bump is part of a stitch pattern. The bar increase is one of the easiest to make and is usually a favorite with knitters. To make it, knit the front loop, but don't remove the stitch from the left needle *(fig. 16b)*. Knit into the back loop of the same stitch *(fig.16c)*.

Make One (m1) These increases are made simply by knitting into the horizontal strand between stitches on the right and left needles. One method creates a left-leaning increase, meaning that the front strand of the increase slants to the left. The other method leans to the right. This is called **paired increases**.

Increases

Yarn Over

Fig. 16a

Knit 1 in the Front and Back Loops

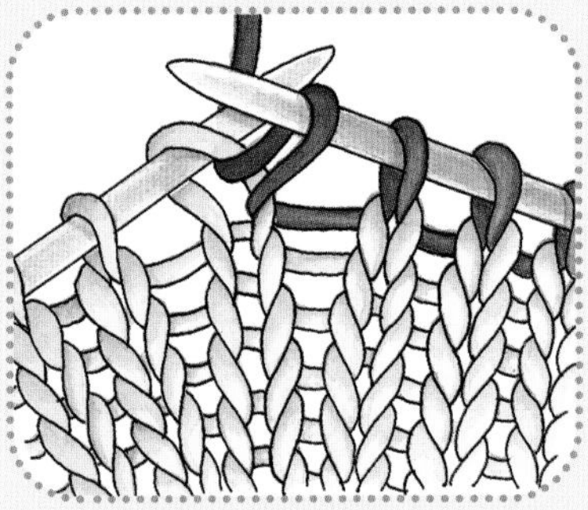

Fig. 16b

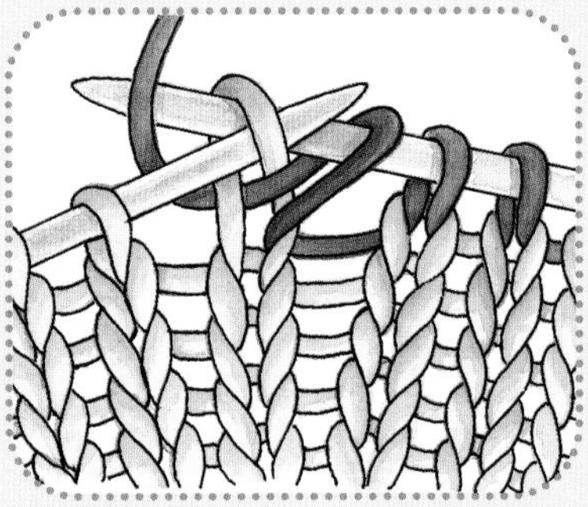

Fig. 16c

Left-leaning Increase

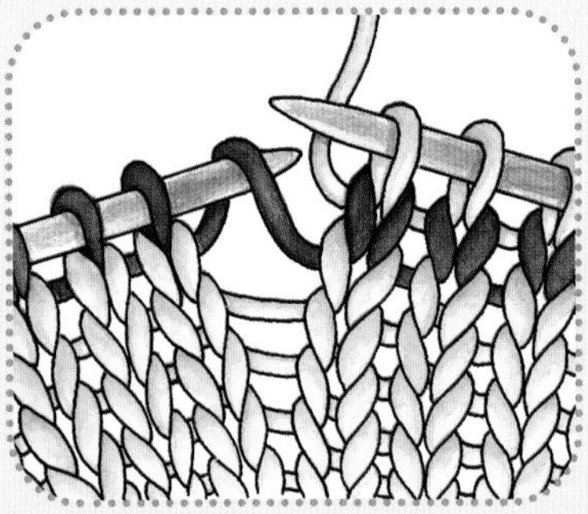

Fig. 16d

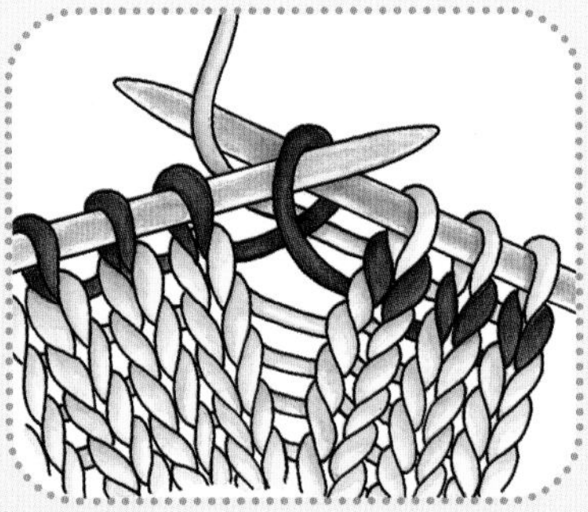

Fig. 16e

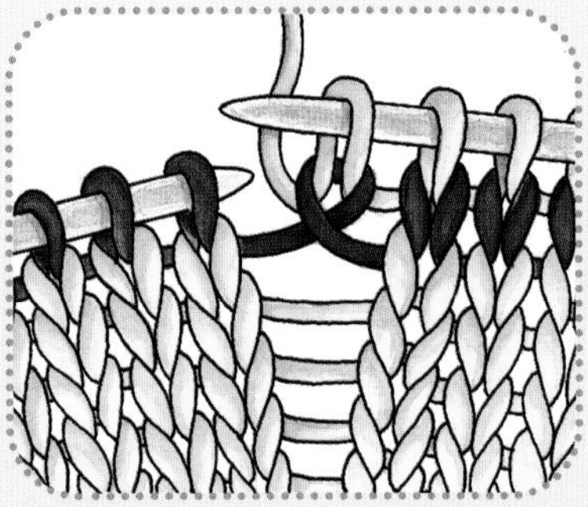

Fig. 16f

Right-leaning Increase

Fig. 16g

Fig. 16h

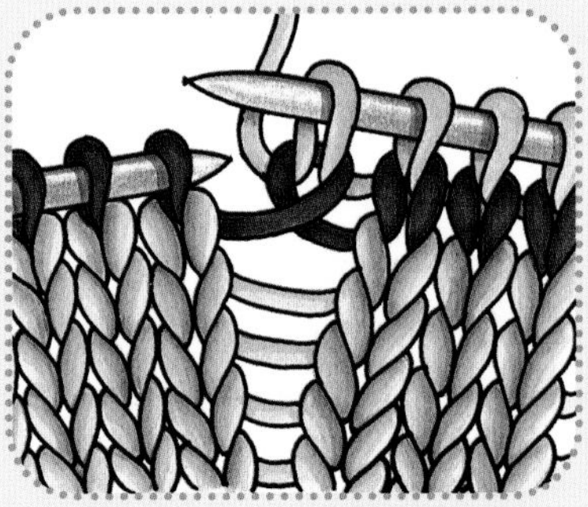

Fig. 16i

Decreases

Knit Two Together

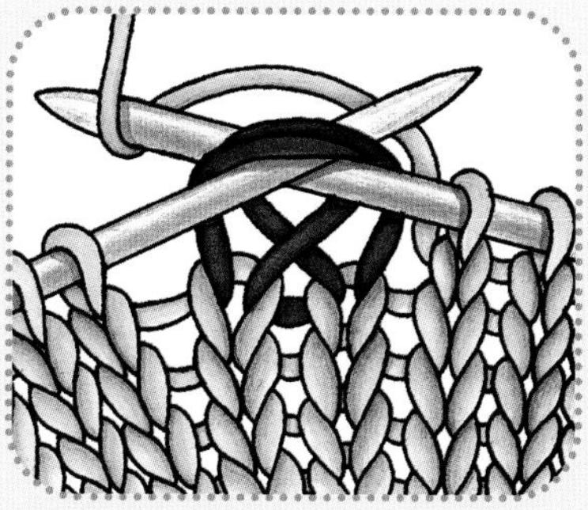

Purl Two Together

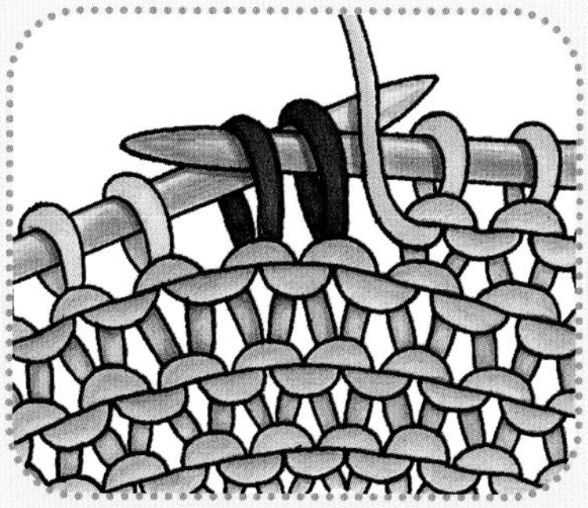

Slip Slip Knit

Fig. 17a

Fig. 17b

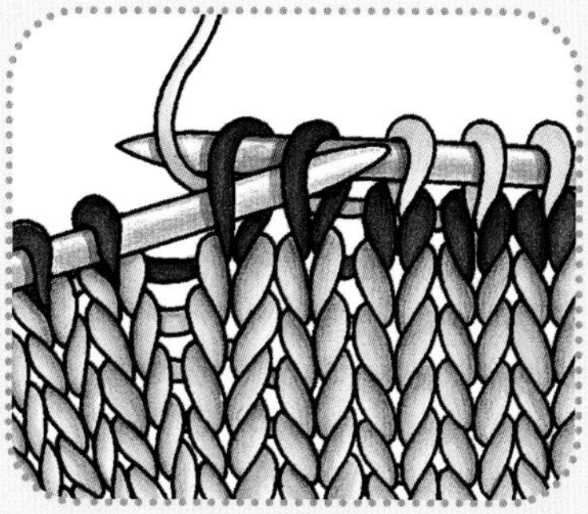

Fig. 17c

To make a left-leaning increase:
Step 1: Insert the left needle from **front to back** under the strand *(fig. 16d)*.
Step 2: With the right needle, knit into the back of the strand *(fig. 16e)*.
Step 3: Slip the strand off the left needle. You now have 1 new stitch (an increase) on the right needle. Note how the front strand of this new stitch leans toward the left *(fig. 16f)*.

To make a right-leaning increase:
Step 1: Insert the left needle from **back to front** under the strand *(fig. 16g)*.
Step 2: Knit into the front of the strand *(fig. 16h)*.
Step 3: Slip the strand off the left needle. You now have 1 new stitch (an increase) on the right needle. Note how the front strand leans toward the right *(fig. 16i)*.

Decreases (dec)

Use **decreases** for shaping the necklines of sweaters, making lace patterns, and many more things. Some decreases have a definite slant either left or right; pattern instructions sometimes specify which type you should use. Left- and right-slant decreases are referred to as **paired decreases.**

Knit Two Together (k2tog) The knit two together decrease is made by

working into two stitches at the same time. With yarn behind your work, skip the first stitch on the left needle and insert the right needle knitwise into the second stitch and the first stitch at the same time. Knit the two stitches as if they were one stitch *(fig. 17a)*, and remove the stitches from the left needle. This decrease leans to the right on the knit side of the work.

Purl Two Together (p2tog) As the name suggests, this decrease is the purl-side method of the knit two together increase. With yarn in front of the work, insert the right needle through the loops of the next two stitches on the left needle as if to purl *(fig. 17b)*; purl the two stitches as if they were one stitch, and remove the stitches from the left needle. This decrease leans to the right when viewed from the knit side.

Slip Slip Knit (ssk) Slip slip knit is a one-stitch decrease that leans to the left and is usually paired with knit two together on knit rows.

Work this decrease as follows: Slip two stitches knitwise, *one at a time,* from the left needle onto the right needle; insert the left needle tip from left to right into the front loops of both slipped stitches *(fig. 17c)* with yarn in back. Knit both stitches together from this position.

Cables

You have probably admired heavily textured Aran sweaters but thought such complicated patterns were beyond your skill level. Although an Aran design is not a good choice for your first project, it *is* something you'll be able to accomplish after honing your skills. One of the main features of an Aran design is the **cable.**

Cables are usually made on a background of reverse stockinette stitch because the bumpy background enhances the smooth cable twists. A cable is basically stitches crossed over each other on the right side of the work; they twist to the right or the left depending on whether you cross to the front or the back of the work. You will need a **cable needle** (see page 8). You can use stitch markers to set off the stitches to be cabled, or you can just read your stitches (know the difference between the reverse stockinette background and the stockinette stitches of the cable) to see where to work the cable. Cables are worked over varying numbers of stitches, usually in stockinette stitch. One of the most common cables is based on four stitches.

Back Cross Cable, or Cable 4 Back (C4b) The four-stitch back cable

Back Cross Cable

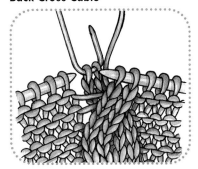

Fig. 18a

Front Cross Cable

Fig. 18b

slants, or crosses, to the right. To make the cable, work to the beginning of the stockinette cable stitches, slip the next two stitches onto the cable needle, and hold it in the back of your work. Knit the next two stitches on the left needle *(fig.18a)*, and then knit the two stitches from the cable needle (C4b made).

Front Cross Cable, or Cable 4 Front (C4f) The four-stitch front cable slants to the left and is made in exactly the same way as the back cable, except that the cable needle is held to the front. Work to the beginning of the stockinette cable stitches, slip the next two stitches onto the cable needle, and hold it in the front of your work. Knit the next two stitches on the left needle *(fig. 18b)*. Knit the two stitches from the cable needle (C4f made).

Stranding Colors
Sometimes called Fair Isle, Scandinavian, or Norwegian knitting, stranding is a technique that allows you to use two colors of yarn on the same row, carrying the yarn not in use across the back of the work *(fig. 19a)*. Fair Isle knitting traditionally uses no more than two colors per row. Scandinavian stranded knitting often uses more than two colors per row. Choose patterns that avoid overly long strands (anything more than an inch worth of stitches). Otherwise, you'll need to weave in the yarn not in use to prevent snags when wearing

the finished product. To weave in, strand the yarn not in use over the working yarn before making the next stitch.

It is possible to knit with the yarn held in one hand, either American-English or Continental style (see page 12), but you can knit much faster and control the tension (uniformity) of the stitches if you learn to knit with a yarn held in each hand *(fig. 19b)*. Not only can you make

Stranding Colors

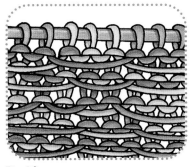

Fig. 19a

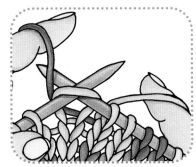

Fig. 19b

Dropped Stitches

Fig. 20a

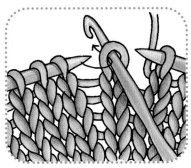

Fig. 20b

beautiful sweaters with this technique, but you can really impress your friends when they see you knitting with both hands!

Important Things to Know
You've learned the basics of knitting—but there's always more to learn. This section helps you polish your skills so that your projects have a professional look.

How to Correct Mistakes
One thing to know about mistakes in knitting is that we *all* make them. Fortunately, knitting is easily corrected, and you'll learn from any missteps. Once you learn to correct them, you'll be happily on your way again.

Dropped Stitches Count your stitches often as you work, especially after casting on and after making increases or decreases. This habit will help you catch many mistakes. If your stitch count is less than it should be, it may be because a stitch has dropped from your needle.

Use a crochet hook to correct a dropped stitch, whether it has dropped one row or several rows (a running stitch).

Step 1: Hold the knit side of the work toward you. Count the horizontal strands between the two needles to determine how many rows the stitch has slipped. It's important to begin with the very first strand closest to the dropped stitch. With the loose horizontal strands behind the loop of the dropped stitch, insert a crochet hook into the loop from front to back. Catch the first horizontal strand and pull it through the stitch *(fig. 20a)*. Repeat the step with each horizontal strand until the dropped stitch is back at the current row.

Step 2: Place the stitch on the left needle *untwisted,* with the right loop of the stitch in front of the needle *(fig. 20b)*.

Continue in pattern.

Joining New Yarn

When you near the end of a ball of yarn, try to change to the new yarn at the row edge. This will prevent uneven stitches in the middle of your work and make weaving in the yarn tails much easier, because you can hide them in the seams.

Step 1: Using an overhand knot (to be removed when finishing the item), tie the old and new yarns together close to the needle, leaving a 4- to 6-inch (10–15cm) tail on both yarns.

Step 2: Drop the old yarn, and begin knitting with the new one. Once you are more experienced and feel more comfortable with controlling the yarns, you may choose to omit knotting the yarns together and simply drop the old yarn and start knitting with the new, tightening and securing the yarn tails later.

Another option is to hold the old and new yarn together and knit with

Changing Colors

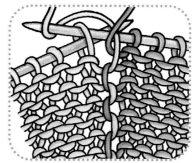

Fig. 21

both for a few stitches. Then drop the old yarn and continue with the new. This method attaches the yarn securely and decreases the number of ends to weave in later, but it can leave a noticeable lump, so don't use it in a prominent place.

Changing Colors When changing colors somewhere other than the end of a row, drop the old color on the wrong side, pick up the new color from underneath the old, and continue knitting with the new color *(fig. 21)*. This prevents a hole from appearing between colors.

How to Make a Simple I-Cord

You can make an I-cord to use as a drawstring, strap, or tie using double-pointed needles or a short circular needle.

Step 1: Cast on 3 or 4 stitches onto one double-pointed needle. Slide the stitches to the other end of the needle. The working yarn is at the "wrong" end of the needle *(fig. 22a)*.

Simple I-Cord

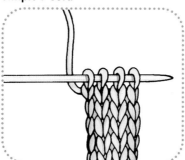

Fig. 22a

Step 2: With the yarn stranded across the back of the stitches, pull it up to the front at the needle tip and knit the stitches*(fig. 22b)*.

Step 3: Repeat step 2 until the cord is the desired length. Unless instructed otherwise, finish the last row as slip 1, knit 2 together, pass the slipped stitch over. Cut the yarn, and thread the end through the last stitch.

Buttonholes

There are many ways to make buttonholes. Three of the most common are the horizontal, the vertical, and the yarn over. The pattern instructions indicate which buttonhole to use, and the materials section lists the number and size of the buttons needed. It's best to buy the buttons before you work the buttonholes so you know exactly what size to make them. Buttonholes in knitting will stretch slightly with wear, so it's a good idea to make the buttonhole slightly smaller than the button. Don't buy buttons with pointed, rough, or sharp edges; they can snag fibers and wear through the yarn very quickly.

Horizontal Buttonhole The horizontal buttonhole is sometimes called the two-row buttonhole because it takes two rows to complete it.

Step 1: On the right side of your knitting, work the specified number of stitches to the beginning of the buttonhole. Then bind off the required number of stitches and continue in

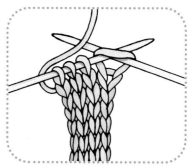

Fig. 22b

Horizontal Buttonhole

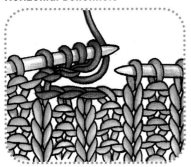

Fig. 23

pattern across the row. (Remember that it takes two stitches to bind off the first stitch.) Count your stitches at the end of the row, subtracting the number you were told to bind off.
Step 2: On the wrong side, work across the row to the bound-off stitches. Cast on the specified number using the simple cast-on *(see figs. 4a, 4b, and 4c, page 11)* or the cable cast-on *(fig. 23)*. Continue in pattern across the row. Count your stitches to make sure you're back to the original stitch count.

Vertical Buttonhole Both sides of this buttonhole are worked at the same time, using separate balls of yarn. If you don't have a spare ball of yarn, wind a small ball before beginning the buttonhole.
Step 1: Working on the wrong-side row and using the working yarn, work across the body of the garment to the desired place for the buttonhole. Drop the working yarn and pick up the new yarn ball. Join the new yarn ball and, beginning with the next stitch, work to the end of the row. The stitch count remains the same.
Step 2: Still using the new yarn, work across to the buttonhole. Drop the new yarn and pick up the working yarn. Using the working yarn, work to the other end of the row. Repeat steps 1 and 2 until the buttonhole is desired length.
Last row: With working yarn, work to the buttonhole and continue to the end of the row. Cut the new yarn, and weave in the loose ends. Continue in pattern, using the working yarn.

Yarn Over Buttonhole This buttonhole is easy to make and is useful for garments, such as baby clothing, that need a small buttonhole. It's also self-enlarging, creating larger buttonholes when thicker yarns are used. It is worked over two stitches as follows: Work to where you want the buttonhole, then work yarn over (yo), knit two together (k2tog). The stitch count remains the same on this row.

Finishing

Most knitters prefer knitting to sewing seams and weaving in ends, but taking care with these final steps ensures that your knitting is shown off to its best both on the outside and the inside.

Picking Up Stitches

Pick up stitches using a knitting needle or crochet hook, and yarn. For a neater edge, use needles or a hook one or two sizes smaller than the working needle. After the pickup is finished, change to the needle size indicated in the instructions. The right side of the work is facing, unless instructed otherwise. If the number of stitches to pick up aren't included in the instructions, measure the area of pickup, and multiply that number by the stitch gauge of the border pattern to be applied. Divide the area of pickup into quarter sections, or smaller spaces if necessary, and mark with pins or thread. This will help you maintain the same number of stitches in each. Example: Pick up and knit 100 stitches. Divide the area into fourths, and pick up 25 stitches in each quarter section. If the border uses a different color than the pickup area, pick up the stitches in the main color, then change to the new color on the next row.

Picking Up Stitches Along a Bound-off Edge With the right side of the garment facing you, insert the tip of the right-hand needle into the *first full stitch* beneath the bind-off row *(fig.*

Picking Up Stitches

Along a Bound-off Edge

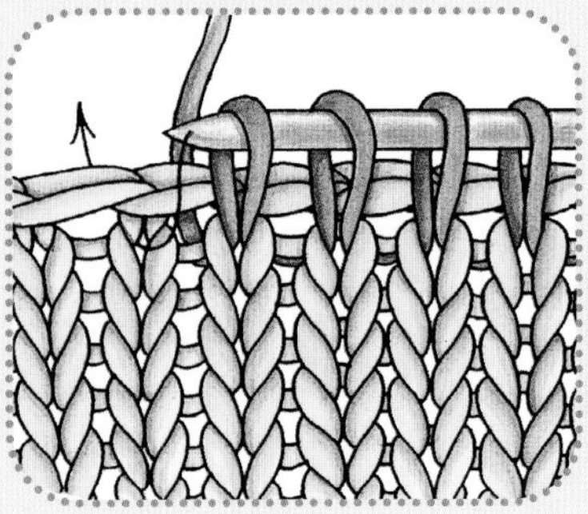

Fig. 24a

Along a Side Edge

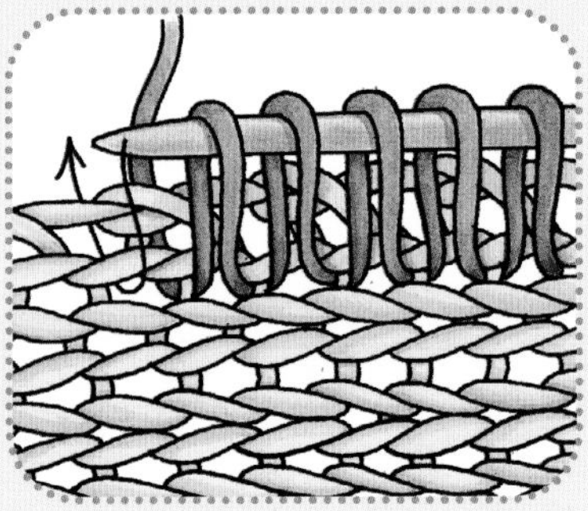

Fig. 24b

Along a Curved Edge

Fig. 24c

24a), wrap the yarn around the needle, and pull it through the stitch, creating a new stitch on the needle. Repeat in each stitch until the required number of stitches are on the needle.

Picking Up Stitches Along a Side Edge

With right side facing, unless instructed otherwise, join the working yarn at the lower edge if not already attached (see Joining New Yarn, page 21). Insert the right needle into the fabric through the first full stitch of the first row and wrap the yarn around the needle knitwise. Pull through a loop, creating a new stitch on the right needle *(fig. 24b)*. Repeat the process, spacing the pickup stitches along the side edge as necessary, but always working into a full stitch. What's important is to not leave any holes or uneven spaces in the work. It's sometimes better to pick up more stitches than indicated, and then decrease the extra stitches evenly across the first row. You may want to practice stitch pickup along the side edges of your gauge swatch before picking up stitches on the actual garment.

Picking Up Stitches Along a Curved Edge

Curved edges are usually a combination of edges...horizontal, diagonal, and vertical. To pick up stitches along an edge that was formed by making decreases, such as along the neck shaping of a sweater, insert the needle into the stitch below the edge stitch *(fig. 24c)*—not between the stitches—to prevent holes from occurring when the pickup is finished.

Sewing Seams

While it may be tempting to hurry through the finishing so you can finally see the completed project, it's important not to rush through sewing the seams if you want the end result to look polished and professional. Block each piece before assembling, and allow the pieces to dry. This helps the edges remain flat as you work.

Shoulder Seams (bound-off edges)

Step 1: Lay both pieces flat, with right sides facing up. Thread a yarn needle, and, beginning at the right-side edge of the piece closest to you (the lower piece), insert the needle from back to front through the center of the first stitch. Pull the yarn through, leaving a yarn tail to weave in later.

Step 2: Insert the needle from right to left under the two vertical legs of the first stitch on the piece farther from you *(fig. 25a)*, then insert the needle from right to left under the next two vertical legs on the near piece, beginning in the same hole as the first stitch was made. Pull the yarn gently to adjust the stitch and close the stitches together.

Step 3: Continue to alternate sides, inserting the needle from right to left under two strands and beginning in the same hole as the last stitch was made. Pull the yarn every few stitches to adjust it and close the seam. At the end of the seam, weave in the yarn tail.

Mattress Stitch Mattress stitch is a great stitch to know when it comes to sewing vertical seams, including side and sleeve seams.

Step 1: Thread a yarn needle with matching color yarn, leaving a four-inch tail to weave in later. With both

Shoulder Seams

Fig. 25a

Mattress Stitch

Fig. 25b

pieces flat and right sides facing up, insert the needle under the horizontal strand between the first and second stitches of the first row on one piece and the corresponding strand on the second piece. Gently pull the yarn to tighten.

Step 2: Insert the needle under the horizontal strand on the next row of one piece, and then insert the needle under the strand on the same row of the other piece.

Step 3: Continue to work under the horizontal strands, alternating pieces, until you have six to eight rows worked *(fig. 25b)*, and then pull the yarn gently to close the seam.

Step 4: Continue weaving together to the end of the seam. Weave yarn tails into the seam stitches, and secure.

Backstitch Backstitch is an easy way to make a firm seam.

Step 1: Thread a tapestry needle with matching yarn. With right sides together, work along the wrong sides about one stitch in from the edges. Work two running stitches on top of each other to secure the lower edges *(see fig. 26a, page 24)*.

Step 2: With the needle and yarn behind the work, insert the needle through both layers of fabric about two stitches to the left of the running stitch and pull the yarn to the front of the work.

Step 3: Insert the needle from front to back one stitch back to the right, working through both layers.

Backstitch

Fig. 26a

Kitchener Stitch

Fig. 28a

Fig. 28b

Step 4: Moving forward to the left about two stitches, bring the needle to the front of the work, about one stitch ahead of the original stitch. Repeat the process until you reach the end of the seam, working one stitch backward (to the right) on the front side of the work and two stitches forward (to the left) on the back side of the work.

Step 5: Finish the seam by working two or three running stitches on top of each other, stitching over the bound-off edges. Weave in yarn tails.

Three-Needle Bind-off This bind-off finishes off two edges, binding off the stitches and closing the seam at the same time. Normally used to close shoulders, it can also be used to close side seams when working a garment from side to side. You can also pick up stitches along two side edges and then use the three-needle bind-off to close those seams. To make a flat, neat seam on the right side, follow these instructions.

Fig. 28c

Fig. 28d

Step 1: With the right sides of the work together, and with the needle tips aligned and facing to the right *(fig. 27a)*, hold both needles in your left hand.

Step 2: Insert the empty right-hand needle into the first stitch on each of the two needles in the left hand, and knit the two stitches together *(fig. 27b)*. Slip them off the needle as you would a knit stitch. You now have one stitch on the right needle.

Step 3: Knit the next pair of stitches the same way. You now have two stitches on the right needle.

Step 4: Pull the first stitch on the right-hand needle over the second stitch (the one closest to the tip), just as you would in a normal bind-off *(fig. 27c)*.

Step 5: Repeat steps 3 and 4 until all stitches have been bound off. Cut the yarn and pull the end through the last loop; weave in the end to secure.

Kitchener Stitch (or Grafting) This technique joins live stitches together in an elastic, invisible seam. The method can also be used over bound-off stitches to make a strong, stable seam.

Three-Needle Bind-off

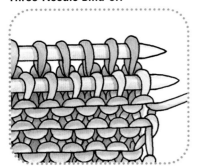

Fig. 27a

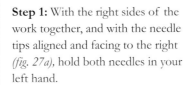

Fig. 27b

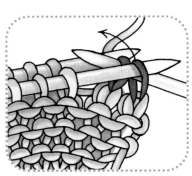

Fig. 27c

With an equal number of stitches on two needles, and right sides facing up, hold the needles parallel to each other with points facing right. Thread a blunt tapestry needle with two to three times the length of the area to be joined. For live stitches, work as follows:

Step 1: Insert threaded needle into the first stitch on the front needle **purlwise** (as if to purl); leave stitch **on** needle.

Step 2: Insert needle into the first stitch on the back needle **knitwise** (as if to knit); leave stitch **on** needle.

Step 3: Insert needle into the same first stitch on the front needle **knitwise** *(fig. 28a);* slip stitch **off** needle. Insert needle into the next front stitch **purlwise;** leave stitch **on** needle *(fig. 28b).*

Step 4: Insert needle into the same stitch on the back needle **purlwise** *(fig. 28c);* slip stitch **off** needle. Insert needle into the next **back** stitch **knitwise;** leave stitch **on** needle *(fig. 28d).*

Repeat steps 3 and 4 until all stitches are worked.

Tip: To make the technique easier as you work, remember this... *Front needle:* purlwise leave on, knitwise take off. *Back needle:* knitwise leave on, purlwise take off.

Weaving in Yarn Tails

Carefully weaving in the yarn ends makes your knitting look neat and keeps it from pulling loose and unraveling over time.

Thread a tapestry needle with the yarn tail. Working on the wrong side of the knitting, weave the needle in and out of the back of the stitches for a few inches in one direction, and then turn and work in the opposite direction for an inch or two. Pull the yarn gently to tighten, and cut it close to the work. Stretch the knitting slightly so that the tail disappears into the last stitch.

Duplicate Stitch

Duplicate stitch is used to create small motifs, make small additions to intarsia (working large patches of color), mend socks, and cover knitting errors. It produces a stiff fabric, as stitches are duplicated on top of the knit fabric below. The technique is worked horizontally, vertically, and diagonally.

For horizontal stitches:

Step 1: Thread a tapestry needle with the same yarn type as the knit fabric beneath. Work with strands about 18″ (46cm) long to avoid having the yarn plies untwist and fibers shed as the needle is drawn through the knit fabric many times. Rethread the tapestry needle as necessary.

Step 2: Begin the first duplicate stitch in the lower right corner of the motif or pattern. (You'll work from right to left.) Secure the yarn on the wrong side of the fabric, and bring the needle through to the front of the fabric at the base of the first stitch.

Step 3: Insert the needle into the right-hand side of the top of the same stitch, carry the needle and yarn across the back of the work, and bring them to the front on the left side of the same stitch *(fig. 29a).* Reinsert the needle into the base of the first stitch.

Step 4: Bring the needle up through the base of the stitch to the left of the stitch just duplicated. Repeat step 3. To work the next horizontal row, insert the needle into the base of the

last horizontal stitch worked, and then bring needle and yarn out to the front through the center of that stitch. Turn the work (the motif will be upside down), and work horizontal stitches across the second row of motif stitches, working the same as the previous row. Continue working horizontal stitches from right to left on each row. Weave the yarn tails through the backs of stitches to secure.

For vertical stitches, begin at the lowest point and work upward. Work the same way as for horizontal duplicate stitch, but bring the needle out to the front through the center of the stitch above the one just worked rather than the stitch to the left *(fig. 29b).*

Diagonal stitches are made using a combination of horizontal and vertical methods. Work one stitch horizontally, and instead of finishing by moving to the next stitch on the left in the same row, bring the needle out at the base of the next stitch on the left, one row above.

Crochet

Knowing how to work a few basic crochet stitches is very useful in knitting. **Chain stitch** (ch), **single crochet** (sc), and **double crochet** (dc) are frequently used by knitters to create decorative edges, to cast on or bind off, and to make buttonholes, buttons, accessory cords, embellishments, and more. Hook

Duplicate Stitch

Fig. 29a

Fig. 29b

Crochet Chain

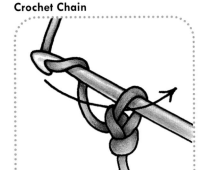

Fig. 30a

Fig. 30b

sizes are coordinated with knitting needle sizes, but the system for labeling size is different. Crochet hooks are numbered in several different ways. The smallest sizes are steel hooks, which use numbers. The higher the number, the smaller the hook size. Larger hooks are labeled with letters and numbers, A/0 through P/16. Some brands also include metric sizes. Many knitters use a hook one or two sizes smaller than their needle size to prevent the crochet from becoming ruffled or wavy instead of lying flat and smooth against the knit fabric. Practice on your gauge swatch to determine which size hook works best on your project.

Crochet Chain (ch)

The chain stitch forms the foundation row in crochet. It is quick and easy to make.

Step 1: Begin with a slipknot. Insert the crochet hook into the center of the slipknot from right to left, catching the working yarn. Pull up a loop, and place it on the crochet hook. Pull both the yarn tail and the working yarn to snug up the slipknot loop around the shank of the crochet hook.

Step 2: Holding the hook in your right hand and the working yarn in your left hand, bring the yarn over the hook from back to front, and pull it through the loop on the crochet hook *(fig. 30a)*.

Step 3: Repeat step 2 until the chain is the desired length *(fig. 30b)*. When the last chain is made, cut the working yarn, leaving a tail to weave in later.

Step 4: Thread the tail through the last chain on the hook, and pull to tighten and secure.

Single Crochet (sc)

Single crochet can be used as a quick and easy finishing edge on your knitted pieces. It is attached either directly to knit stitches, along a bound-off edge, or as a border for other crochet stitches. It makes a firm finish and helps the edges to lay flat.

Step 1: Insert the hook under a bound-off stitch (or wherever directed in the instructions). Bring the working yarn over the hook and pull through a loop, yarn over again, and pull it through the loop on the hook *(fig. 31a)*.

Step 2: Insert the hook under the next bound-off stitch *(fig. 31b)*, yarn over, and pull up a loop (two loops on hook). Yarn over again, and pull the yarn back through both loops on the hook, leaving one loop on the hook *(fig. 31c)*.

Step 3: Repeat step 2 until the required number of stitches is completed. Finish according to pattern instructions.

Double Crochet (dc)

This stitch is worked into a chain, single crochet, or directly into the knitting, as shown here.

Step 1: Insert the hook into the knitting one stitch in from the edge, yarn over and draw up a loop. Yarn over again, and pull it through the loop on the hook. Yarn over, insert the hook into the next base stitch *(fig. 32a)*, and draw up a loop (three loops on hook). Yarn over and pull it through the first two loops *(fig. 32b)*,

Single Crochet

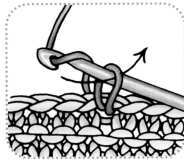

Fig. 31a

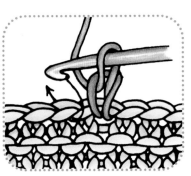

Fig. 31b

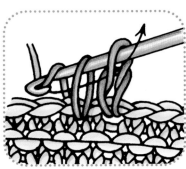

Fig. 31c

Double Crochet

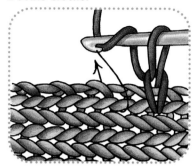

Fig. 32a

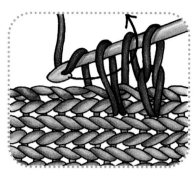

Fig. 32b

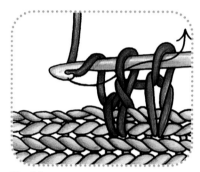

Fig. 32c

Fig. 32d

yarn over and pull it through the last two loops *(fig. 32c)*.

The double crochet is complete; one loop is on the hook *(fig. 32d)*. **Step 2:** Yarn over, insert the hook in the next stitch, yarn over, and pull up a loop (three loops on hook). Yarn over and pull it through two loops, yarn over and pull it through the remaining two loops. The second double crochet is complete, with one loop left on the hook.

Repeat step 2 for pattern. To end the last stitch, after completing step 2, cut the yarn and pull it through the last loop on the hook.

Washing and Blocking

Always save at least one label from your yarn when you make an item that needs to be washed often. Keep it where you can easily find it when it's time to wash the piece. Some yarns can be safely washed in the washing machine and dried in the dryer, but others would be destroyed by such treatment. If you have any doubt, play it safe—hand-wash it.

Fill a sink with lukewarm water (never hot!), and add a small amount of mild soap made especially for delicate knits. Put the garment in the sink, and allow it to soak. *Do not* agitate or handle roughly, or felting could begin (see Felting, next). Drain the sink, and gently press down on the garment to squeeze some of the water out. Never wring or twist a wet item; always support the weight so the item doesn't stretch. Fill the sink with cool rinse water; allow the item to soak, drain the water, and again gently press out the excess water. Repeat until the soap is removed.

Have a blocking board (a thick, padded board on which to pin damp garments so they can dry to the correct size) ready, or spread a layer of thick towels on a flat surface such as a table or a bed. (Never hang a knitted garment.) Lift the garment from the sink with both hands without stretching it, and spread it out on the prepared surface. Use a tape measure to shape it to the correct measurements. Pin in place using rustproof T-pins, and let dry.

Some yarns, including wool, can be blocked by using steam, but always check the yarn label first. Lay the garment on a blocking board, and pin it to the correct measurements. Keep the steam spray several inches above the garment—never put it directly on to the garment.

Felting (or Fulling)

Felting is the process of using hot water, agitation, and suds to change (or shrink) a knitted piece into a felted fabric that will not unravel, even when cut. Felting creates a very durable fabric that is practical as well as beautiful.

When making an item to be felted, use extra-large needles and make it several sizes larger than normal. This creates space between the stitches and rows and allows the fibers to shrink while maintaining a smooth fabric surface.

Animal fibers are best for felting. You can use wool, mohair, camel, and alpaca, among others. Superwash wool yarns have been treated to resist shrinking—they will not felt. Synthetic yarns do not felt, either.

To felt, set the washing machine on the hot water cycle and low water level. Add a small amount of dishwashing liquid; too many suds hampers the felting process. Add towels, tennis balls, or washable sneakers to the machine to balance the load and aid the felting process. Allow the machine to agitate for five minutes, then stop it to check the amount of felting. Continue to check every five minutes or so until the stitches completely disappear and the item is the desired size. The amount of felting time varies depending upon yarn, washing machine, and hardness of water.

Once the desired felting stage is obtained, remove the item from the washing machine, drain the soapy water, and fill it with cold rinse water. Soak the item in rinse water for several minutes to remove all soapiness. Set the machine directly on spin cycle to eliminate excess water from the felted item, or wrap it in a large towel and squeeze to take out the rinse water. Remove the felted item from the machine *immediately* after spinning to avoid wrinkling the fabric. Stretch, pull, and pat it into shape, and allow it to air-dry on a flat surface.

Understanding Knitting Instructions

Like most crafts, knitting has its own language. Knitting patterns use abbreviations, special terms, and punctuation. Knitting language may seem strange and a little intimidating at first, but you will quickly master it and be reading patterns like a pro.

At the beginning of each pattern in this book, you'll find a list of techniques used in that project. Review the techniques listed, and when you see one you don't know, turn to the page referenced and practice the technique before starting the pattern.

Return to the pattern you plan to make, and read any special notes or instructions. Locate the size you want to make, and circle it throughout the pattern. Or make a copy of the pattern, and highlight the correct size numbers. In most patterns, the size numbers list the smallest size first, with the other sizes listed within brackets, beginning with the next size up, and so on. When one number or set of instructions is given, it applies to all sizes.

When a Finished Size is listed, the numbers given refer to the garment size upon completion (provided you maintain the correct gauge). These measurements include garment ease. Some patterns include both the body size and a finished size. For example:
Bust size: 36″ [38″, 40″]
Finished size: 40″ [42″, 44″]

Standard Knitting Abbreviations

Use this key as a reference for new and unfamiliar abbreviations. To simplify instructions for the beginning knitter, however, this book spells out all knitting terms within the instructions, although common abbreviations are included in the Techniques section of each pattern.

[ ]	Work instructions within brackets as many times as directed
( )	Work instructions within parentheses in the place directed
*	Repeat instructions following the asterisk as directed
* to **	Repeat instructions between the * and ** as directed
alt	alternate
approx	approximate
beg	beginning/begin
bet	between
BO	bind off
CO	cast on
cont	continue
dec	decrease/decreases/decreasing
dpn	double-pointed needles
foll	follow/follows/following
g st	garter stitch
inc	increase/increases/increasing
k or K	knit
k1,p1	knit 1, purl 1
k2tog	knit 2 together
kwise	knitwise
LH	left-hand
m1	make 1 stitch
m1 p-st	make 1 purl stitch
p or P	purl
p2tog	purl 2 stitches together
pm	place marker
prev	previous
psso	pass slipped stitch over
pwise	purlwise
rem	remain/remaining
rep	repeat(s)
rev St st	reverse stockinette stitch
RH	right-hand
rnd(s)	round(s)
RS	right side
sk	skip
skp	slip, knit, pass slipped stitch over—1 stitch decreased
sk2p	slip 1, knit 2 together, pass slipped stitch over the knit 2 together—2 stitches decreased
sl	slip
sl1k	slip 1 knitwise
sl1p	slip 1 purlwise
sl st	slip stitch
ssk	slip, slip, knit these 2 stitches together—a decrease
sssk	slip, slip, slip, knit these 3 stitches together—a 2-stitch decrease
st(s)	stitch(es)
St st	stockinette stitch
tbl	through back loop
tog	together
WS	wrong side
wyib	with yarn in back
wyif	with yarn in front
yfwd	yarn forward
yo	yarn over
yon	yarn over needle

Reading through the entire pattern may be confusing at first, so study small sections. If the pattern begins with the Back, read through those instructions to make sure you understand what will happen, then make the Back. Read through the next section, then knit it, and so on.

Pay attention to punctuation. One sentence usually represents one row; commas and semicolons may mean that something's going to change with the next stitch or row. Instructions inside asterisks, brackets, or parentheses are usually repeated, so look for the directions that explain what to do.

Schematics

These are line drawings of the basic garment pieces, to which measurements are added. Usually schematics show the basic measurements before neck ribbing, collars, or other embellishments are added. Check the schematic to determine which size will best fit you in width and length.

Home Decor

Luxurious throws, personal touches, festive decorations…hand-knit decorative accents can really make a house a home. This chapter includes some very easy patterns, making it a good place for new knitters to embark on their knitting journey.

Designer Dishcloths

Making dishcloths is a great way for a knitting novice to practice new stitch patterns. These projects are quick, fun to make, and useful. Try the three patterns shown here, and beware: They're habit-forming!

Designer: Lucie Sinkler

Techniques
Binding off—BO (page 14)
Casting on—CO (page 9)
Garter stitch (page 15)
Knit stitch–k (page 12)
Purl stitch–p (page 13)
Weaving in yarn tails (page 25)

Size
9×11″ (23×28cm)

⊛ ⊛ ⊛

Gauge
Blue dishcloth:
19 stitches/32 rows=4″ (10cm)
in pattern

Yellow dishcloth:
18 stitches/28 rows=4″ (10cm)
in pattern

Multicolor dishcloth:
19 stitches/33 rows=4″ (10cm)
in pattern

Note: Exact gauge isn't necessary; the finished dishcloths will either be slightly smaller or larger if your gauge is a bit off.

⊛ ⊛ ⊛

What You'll Need
Yarn: Worsted weight cotton yarn, about 75 yards (69m) for each dishcloth **We used:** Lily Sugar'n Cream (100% cotton): #26 Light Blue, 1 ball; #86 Lemon Chiffon, 1 ball; Lily Sugar'n Cream Crafter's Cotton (100% cotton): #201 Cool Breeze, 1 ball

Needles: US size 7 (4.5mm)

Notion: Tapestry needle

Make the blue dishcloth
Cast on 43 stitches.

Row 1: Knit 3, *purl 1, knit 3**; repeat from * to ** to end of row.

Row 2: Knit.

Repeat rows 1 and 2 until piece measures 11″ (28cm). Bind off. See Finishing, below.

Make the yellow dishcloth
Cast on 42 stitches. Knit in garter stitch (knit every row) for 6 rows.

Begin main pattern

Row 1: Knit.

Row 2: Knit 4, purl 34, knit 4.

Row 3: Knit 4, purl 5, [knit 4, purl 6] 2 times, knit 4, purl 5, knit 4.

Row 4: Knit 4, purl 34, knit 4.

Row 5: Knit.

Row 6: Knit 4, purl 34, knit 4.

Row 7: Knit 8, [purl 6, knit 4] 3 times, knit 4.

Row 8: Knit 4, purl 34, knit 4.

Repeat these 8 rows for pattern. Work even until piece measures about 10¼″ (26cm), ending with row 8. Knit 6 rows in garter stitch. Bind off. See Finishing, below.

Make the multicolor dishcloth
Cast on 43 stitches.

Row 1: [Knit 1, purl 1] across row. Repeat for desired length, beginning each row with a knit stitch to create seed-stitch pattern. Bind off. See Finishing, below.

Finishing
Cut yarn, leaving about 6″ (15cm) tail. Thread tapestry needle, and secure yarn by weaving across a few stitches on wrong side of work.

How to Care for Hand-knit Dishcloths
Machine-wash or hand-wash them in cold water using mild soap. Do not bleach. Rinse well in cold water. Squeeze gently, and roll in a towel to remove excess water. Reshape and lay flat to dry. Wash dark colors separately.

Mixed Fiber Throw

A blend of fabulous textures and yarn weights gives this easy-to-knit throw its own special look and feel. Working it widthwise rather than lengthwise adds a special and unusual twist.

Designer: Lisa Daniels

Techniques

Binding off—BO (page 14)
Casting on—CO (page 9)
Joining new yarn (page 21)
Knit stitch—k (page 12)
Purl stitch—p (page 13)

Size

About 60×40" (152.5×101.5cm)

⊛　⊛　⊛

Gauge

14 stitches=6" (15cm)

⊛　⊛　⊛

What You'll Need

Yarn: A mixture of several bulky and other yarns in natural fibers: 8oz (227g) mohair; 4oz (114g) merino ribbon; 8oz (227g) blend mohair and nylon; 8oz (227g) mohair and wool; 3.5oz (100g) eyelash-type yarn of mohair and nylon

We used: Mountain Colors Mohair (78% mohair, 13% wool, 9% nylon): Northern Lights, 2 skeins; Mountain Colors Merino Ribbon (80% kid mohair, 20% nylon): Northern Lights, 1 skein; Mountain Colors Moguls (96% mohair, 4% nylon): Northern Lights, 2 skeins; Mountain Colors Mountain Goat (55% mohair, 45% wool): Northern Lights, 2 skeins; Mountain Colors Wooly Feathers (65% kid mohair, 35% nylon): Northern Lights, 1 skein

Needles: US size 11 (8mm)

Notion: Tapestry needle

Stitch pattern

Row 1: Purl.
Rows 2 and 3: Knit.
Row 4: Purl.

Yarn sequence key

1: Mohair yarn: Work 4 rows of stitch pattern as listed above.
2: Merino Ribbon yarn: Work 4 rows of stitch pattern.
3: Mohair yarn: Work 4 rows of stitch pattern.
4: Moguls yarn: Work 4 rows of stitch pattern.
5: Mohair yarn: Work 4 rows of stitch pattern.
6: Mountain Goat yarn (use 2 strands held together as 1): Work 4 rows of stitch pattern.

The above 24 rows are the yarn sequence. When instructions specify to begin Yarn Sequence, work these same 24 rows, in the order of yarns as listed, unless instructed otherwise.

Make the throw

This throw is worked by casting on the length and working across the width.

Border: Cast on 135 stitches with Mountain Goat (used doubled). Work rows 3 and 4 of stitch pattern. Change to Wooly Feathers, and work rows 1–4 of stitch pattern.

Yarn Sequences 1, 2, 3: Work the 24 rows as listed in yarn sequence key a total of 3 times. (78 rows from cast-on edge at this point: 6 rows of border plus 72 rows of 3 yarn sequences)

Yarn Sequence 4 only: Work the 24-row yarn sequence as before, *with 1 difference:* Substitute Wooly Feathers for Yarn #4, Moguls. (102 rows from cast-on edge)

Yarn Sequences 5, 6, 7: Work 3 full sequences of stitch pattern using the yarns as listed in yarn sequence key (174 rows from cast-on edge). With #1, Mohair, work rows 1–4 of stitch pattern.

Border: With Wooly Feathers, work rows 1–4 of stitch pattern. With Mountain Goat (used doubled), work rows 1 and 2 of stitch pattern.

Next row: Bind off all stitches loosely. Weave in all loose ends to wrong side of work.

Padded Hanger and Sachet

Dress up an old hanger in an instant with this easy project. Fill the cute little sachet with your favorite dried flowers, aromatic herbs, potpourri, or cedar shavings.

Designer: Lucie Sinkler

Techniques

Binding off—BO (page 14)
Casting on—CO (page 9)
Crochet chain (page 26)
Garter stitch (page 15)
Knit 2 together—k2tog (page 19)
Mattress stitch (page 23)
Weaving in yarn tails (page 25)
Yarn over—yo (page 17)

Size

Hanger cover: about 16″ (40.5cm)
Sachet: 2¾×2¾″ (7×7cm)

Gauge

21 stitches/11 rows=4″ (10cm)
in garter stitch

What You'll Need

Yarn: 60 yards (55m) worsted weight yarn for hanger cover (yarn A); 20 yards (18m) coordinating yarn for sachet (yarn B)
We used: Patons Grace (100% cotton): #60903 lavender (yarn A), 1 ball; #60005 snow (yarn B), 1 ball

Needles: US size 5 (3.75mm)

Notions: Size F/5 (3.75mm) crochet hook; tapestry needle; sewing needle and white sewing thread; ½″ (1.3cm) decorative button

Miscellaneous: straight wooden hanger with metal hook

Make the sachet

Holding 2 strands of yarn B together as 1, cast on 15 stitches. Work in garter stitch (knit every row) for about 5″ (12.5cm).
Next row (eyelet buttonhole): Knit 6, knit 2 together, yarn over, knit 7. Knit 5 more rows; bind off. Fold piece in half, and weave sides together using mattress stitch. Placing seam in middle of back, sew bottom together using mattress stitch.

Crochet chain: Insert crochet hook into 1 side seam, just under top edge. Using 2 strands of yarn B, work a crochet chain for 7″ (18cm). Cut yarn, leaving about 6″ (15cm) tail. With threaded tapestry needle, attach chain to opposite side seam under the top edge and to the inside. Weave yarn ends through several stitches on wrong side of work, and secure. With sewing needle and thread, attach button in position on *inside* of sachet, opposite eyelet buttonhole.

Make the hanger cover

Holding 2 strands of yarn A together as 1, cast on 80 stitches and work in garter stitch (knit every row) for 2¾″ (7cm). Bind off all stitches. Cut yarn, leaving about 30″ (76cm) tail. Find center of knit piece, and slip it over the metal hanger hook, taking care not to snag knitting. Fold knit piece in half lengthwise over hanger. Thread tapestry needle with yarn tail, and weave loose ends to wrong side to secure. Pull yarn snugly to gather and tighten side edge and enclose it over hanger end. Close other side in the same way. Weave loose ends to wrong side and through a few stitches to secure. Sew cast-on and bind-off edges together neatly. Weave last remaining yarn tail to inside, and secure.

 Tip

Two Birds with One Swatch

For this project, you can use almost any medium-weight yarn. Make the sachet first, and use this piece as your gauge swatch. Measure how many stitches fit in 1 inch, and multiply that number by the length of your hanger in inches. That number is the total number of stitches to cast on for the hanger cover.

Americana Pot Holder

This darling pot holder captures the special style of homespun early Americana. The crocheted edge and classic shades of red, white, and blue make the pot holder look special without involving complicated techniques.

Designer: Darlene Hayes

Techniques

Binding off—BO (page 14)
Casting on—CO (page 9)
Crochet chain (page 26)
Garter stitch (page 15)
Single crochet (page 26)

Size

Approximately 7×7″ (18×18cm)

⊗ ⊗ ⊗

Gauge

24 stitches/48 rows=4″ (10cm)
in garter stitch

⊗ ⊗ ⊗

What You'll Need

Yarn: Approximately 100 yards (274m) each 98.3% cotton, 1.7% elastic yarn in 3 colors
We used: Cascade Yarns Fixation: #8176 Ecru (color A), 1 skein; #2625 Blueberry (color B), 1 skein; #3794 Wine (color C), 1 skein

Needles: US size 5 (3.75mm)

Notions: US size G (4.25mm) crochet hook; tapestry needle

Notes:
• Yarn is used doubled throughout. Wind color A into 2 balls before starting.
• Special abbreviation: sl2kp. Slip 2 together as if to knit, knit 1, pass the slipped stitches over (a centered double decrease).

Make the pot holder

Cast on 71 stitches using 2 strands of color A held together as 1. Work as follows:

Row 1: Knit 34, slip 2 stitches together knitwise, knit 1, pass both slipped stitches over the knit stitch, knit 34. (69 stitches)

Row 2 and all even-numbered rows: Knit.

Row 3: Knit 33, sl2kp, knit 33. (67 stitches)

Row 5: Knit 32, sl2kp, knit 32. (65 stitches)

Row 7: Change to colors B and C (1 strand each color held together as 1); knit 31, sl2kp, knit 31. (63 stitches)

Row 9: Knit 30, sl2kp, knit 30. (61 stitches)

Row 11: Knit 29, sl2kp, knit 29. (59 stitches)

Row 13: Knit 28, sl2kp, knit 28. (57 stitches)

Row 15: Knit 27, sl2kp, knit 27. (55 stitches)

Row 17: Knit 26, sl2kp, knit 26. (53 stitches)

Row 19: Change to color A (2 strands held together as 1); knit 25, sl2kp, knit 25. (51 stitches)

Row 21: Knit 24, sl2kp, knit 24. (49 stitches)

Row 23: Knit 23, sl2kp, knit 23. (47 stitches)

Row 25: Knit 22, sl2kp, knit 22. (45 stitches)

Row 27: Knit 21, sl2kp, knit 21. (43 stitches)

Row 29: Knit 20, sl2kp, knit 20. (41 stitches)

Row 31: Knit 19, sl2kp, knit 19. (39 stitches)

Row 33: Change to colors B and C (1 strand each color held together as 1); knit 18, sl2kp, knit 18. (37 stitches)

Row 35: Knit 17, sl2kp, knit 17. (35 stitches)

Row 37: Knit 16, sl2kp, knit 16. (33 stitches)

Row 39: Knit 15, sl2kp, knit 15. (31 stitches)

Row 41: Knit 14, sl2kp, knit 14. (29 stitches)

Row 43: Knit 13, sl2kp, knit 13. (27 stitches)

Row 45: Change to color A (2 strands held together as 1); knit 12, sl2kp, knit 12. (25 stitches)

Row 47: Knit 11, sl2kp, knit 11. (23 stitches)

Row 49: Knit 10, sl2kp, knit 10. (21 stitches)

Row 51: Knit 9, sl2kp, knit 9. (19 stitches)

Row 53: Knit 8, sl2kp, knit 8. (17 stitches)

Row 55: Knit 7, sl2kp, knit 7. (15 stitches)

Row 57: Knit 6, sl2kp, knit 6. (13 stitches)

Bind off remaining 13 stitches. Cut yarn, leaving tails of about 24″ (61cm).

Yards vs. Meters

When the materials list in your pattern lists the amount of yarn needed in yards, but the yarn you want to use is listed in meters, don't fret! There's an easy formula for converting one to the other.

To convert from meters to yards, multiply the meters by 1.09

To convert from yards to meters, multiply the yards by 0.91

Hanging loop: Using crochet hook and yarn tails, make a single chain of 13 stitches, attaching last stitch to other side of pot holder at beginning of bound-off row, forming a loop (see photo). Thread remaining tail end on tapestry needle, and weave between bound-off stitches to secure. With colors B and C held together as 1, join to work at 1 side of loop, and work in single crochet around edge of pot holder, including outside of loop (see photo). Do not work single crochet under loop, across bound-off stitches. Use tapestry needle to weave in all loose ends.

Felted Christmas Stocking

Bring your mantel to life during the holiday season! Select your favorite shade of wool for this elegant stocking, or choose several. Just imagine how festive the mantel will look when you hang a different-color stocking for each member of your family.

Designer: Lucie Sinkler

Techniques

Binding off—BO (page 14)
Casting on—CO (page 9)
Felting (page 27)
Joining new yarn (page 21)
Knit 2 together—k2tog
(page 19)
Picking up stitches (page 22)
Purl 2 together—p2tog
(page 19)
Slip a stitch knitwise, purlwise
(page 17)
Slip slip knit decrease—ssk (page 19)
Stockinette stitch—St st (page 15)
Weaving in yarn tails (page 25)

Size

After felting: 16″ (40.5cm) in length,
11″ (28cm) circumference

✱ ✱ ✱

Gauge

13 stitches=4″ (10cm) in stockinette
stitch, before felting

✱ ✱ ✱

What You'll Need

Yarn: 200 yards (183m) heavy
worsted weight 100% wool yarn for
stocking (*do not use superwash wool for
felting projects*); 50 yards (46m) fuzzy
yarn for trim
We used: Brown Sheep Lambs Pride
(85% wool, 15% mohair):
M145 Spice (yarn A), 2 skeins;
Garnstudio Pelliza (100% polyester):
#5 red (yarn B), 1 ball.

Needles: US size 10½ (6.5mm)

Notions: Tapestry needle;
2 stitch holders

Miscellaneous: Washing machine;
dishwashing liquid

Make the stocking

Cuff: Holding both yarns together as 1, cast on 50 stitches. Purl 1 row. Work in stockinette stitch for 7″ (18cm). End with a knit row. Cut yarn B, leaving a 6″ (15cm) tail; thread tapestry needle and weave tail to wrong side of work.

Stocking leg: Continue stocking with yarn A only. Work in stockinette stitch for 11″ (28cm), measuring from last row of yarn B to the row beneath needle. End with a knit row.

First ½ heel flap: Purl 14 stitches; slip remaining 36 stitches onto stitch holder. Turn and work in stockinette stitch for additional 15 rows, ending with a knit row.

Heel turn: The heel is turned using short rows, which means that some stitches in the row are not worked until later.

Next row (Row 1): Purl 3, purl 2 together, purl 1, turn work (leave remaining 8 stitches on needle).

Row 2 and all right-side rows: Slip first stitch knitwise, knit to end of row.

Row 3: Purl 4, purl 2 together, purl 1, turn work.

Row 5: Purl 5, purl 2 together, purl 1, turn.

Row 7: Purl 6, purl 2 together, purl 1, turn.

Row 9: Purl 7, purl 2 together, purl 1, cut yarn. You will have 9 stitches on the needle. Slip them onto a second stitch holder.

Second ½ heel flap: Starting at other edge of stocking, slip 14 stitches purlwise from first stitch holder onto tapestry needle (leave center 22 stitches on holder). With wrong side facing, rejoin yarn at 14th stitch; purl to end of row. Work in stockinette stitch for additional 14 rows.

Heel turn

Next row (Row 1): Knit 3, slip slip knit decrease, knit 1, turn work (leave remaining 8 stitches on needle).

Row 2 and all wrong-side rows: Slip first stitch purlwise, purl to end.

Row 3: Knit 4, slip slip knit, knit 1, turn.

Row 5: Knit 5, slip slip knit, knit 1, turn.

Row 7: Knit 6, slip slip knit, knit 1, turn.

Row 9: Knit 7, slip slip knit, knit 1 (do not turn). With 9 stitches on needle, pick up 9 stitches along side of heel flap; knit across center 22 stitches from stitch holder; pick up 9 stitches along side of first heel flap; knit remaining 9 stitches from holder. (58 stitches)

Gusset shaping

Row 1 and all odd-number rows: Purl across all stitches.

Row 2: Knit 17, knit 2 together, knit 20, slip slip knit, knit 17.

Row 4: Knit 16, knit 2 together, knit 20, slip slip knit, knit 16.

Row 6: Knit 15, knit 2 together, knit 20, slip slip knit, knit 15.

Row 8: Knit 14, knit 2 together, knit 20, slip slip knit, knit 14.

Row 10: Knit 13, knit 2 together, knit 20, slip slip knit, knit 13. (48 stitches)

Work in stockinette stitch for 5 inches (12.5cm). End with purl row.

Toe shaping

Row 1: [Knit 6, knit 2 together] 6 times. (42 stitches)

Row 2 and all wrong-side rows: Purl.

Row 3: [Knit 5, knit 2 together] 6 times. (36 stitches)

Row 5: [Knit 4, knit 2 together] 6 times. (30 stitches)

Row 7: [Knit 3, knit 2 together] 6 times. (24 stitches)

Row 9: [Knit 2, knit 2 together] 6 times. (18 stitches)

Row 11: [Knit 1, knit 2 together] 6 times. (12 stitches)

Row 13: [Knit 2 together] 6 times. (6 stitches)

Finishing

Cut yarn, leaving 18″ (46cm) tail. Thread tapestry needle, and draw needle and yarn through remaining stitches to close toe. Insert tapestry needle to wrong side of work, and weave yarn tail through several stitches to secure. Fold stocking in half, and sew edges together using simple overcast stitch. (Cut more yarn and rethread needle as necessary.) Fold cuff in half, and sew edge loosely to stocking, working from the inside. Weave in all loose ends to wrong side of work, and secure. Follow felting instructions on page 27 to felt stocking.

The Knitty-Gritty

Colors to Dye For

Have fun dyeing your own yarn with simple and inexpensive things you probably have stocked in your pantry. You can use tea, food coloring, RIT dyes, Easter egg dye tablets—even Kool-Aid soft drink mix. And it's easier than you might think! (Children will love to do this with you, as it's one of the few times they can stain to their heart's content and not get in trouble for it.)

Use wool yarn (acrylics and synthetics won't work as well). Wind the yarn into small hanks or skeins, and fill a stainless-steel or enamel pan with enough warm water to completely cover the yarn. Sprinkle a few packages of Kool-Aid or other dye into the water; stir. Add yarn, and place pan on stove. Heat the water until it just simmers; don't let it boil. Simmer for approximately 30 minutes, stirring occasionally. Turn the heat off, and let the water cool slightly.

Fill a dishpan with warm water and a little mild detergent, and soak the yarn in it for 10 to 20 minutes. Empty the pan, and fill it with clean, warm water. Repeat until the water runs clear. Gently squeeze the excess water from the yarn, and hang the yarn over a dowel, a clothes hanger, or an old curtain rod. Let dry.

Lovely Lace Edging

Add simple knitted lace edging to everyday hand towels, and smile as guests admire your handiwork. These edgings are worked sideways after casting on a few stitches. Work the lace in any length, and apply to pillowcases, afghans, scarves, and more.   Designer: Lucie Sinkler

Gauge

Natural edging on sage towel:
24 stitches/36 rows=4"
(10cm) in pattern

Natural edging on natural towel:
24 stitches/38 rows=4"
(10cm) in pattern

Sage edging on natural towel:
24 stitches/32 rows=4"
(10cm) in pattern

❀ ❀ ❀

What You'll Need

Yarn: 50 yards (46m) sport weight 100% cotton (natural edging on sage towel); 70 yards (63.7m) sport weight 100% cotton (natural edging on natural towel); 70 yards (63.7m) sport weight 100% cotton (sage edging on natural towel)

We used: Needful Yarns Lana Gatto Skipper (100% cotton): #124 natural, 1 ball each for natural edging on natural towel and natural edging on sage towel; #123 sage, 1 ball

Needles: US size 2 (2.75mm)

Notions: Tapestry needle; long pins with large heads; sewing needle and thread to match

Miscellaneous: 16×24" (40.5×61cm) hand towel, or desired size

Natural-color edging on sage towel

Cast on 8 stitches.

Row 1: Knit 3, yarn over, knit 2 together, yarn over, knit 3. (9 stitches)

Rows 2, 4, 6, 8, and 10: Knit.

Row 3: Knit 3, yarn over, knit 2 together, yarn over, knit 4. (10 stitches)

Row 5: Knit 3, yarn over, knit 2 together, yarn over, knit 5. (11 stitches)

Row 7: Knit 3, yarn over, knit 2 together, yarn over, knit 6. (12 stitches)

Row 9: Knit 3, yarn over, knit 2 together, yarn over, knit 7. (13 stitches)

Row 11: Knit 3, yarn over, knit 2 together, yarn over, knit 8. (14 stitches)

Row 12: Bind off 6 stitches, knit to the end of the row. (8 stitches)

Repeat rows 1–12 for pattern. Continue in pattern until the edging, when slightly stretched, fits across bottom edge of towel. Complete edging, binding off all stitches at row 12. See Finishing, page 44.

Natural-color edging on natural towel

Cast on 12 stitches.

Row 1: Knit 4, yarn over, knit 2 together, knit 2, yarn over, knit 2 together, yarn over, knit 2. (13 stitches)

Row 2: Yarn over, knit 2 together, knit 11.

Row 3: Knit 3, [yarn over, knit 2 together] 2 times, knit 2, yarn over, knit 2 together, yarn over, knit 2. (14 stitches)

Row 4: Yarn over, knit 2 together, knit 12.

Row 5: Knit 4, [yarn over, knit 2 together] 2 times, knit 2, yarn over, knit 2 together, yarn over, knit 2. (15 stitches)

Row 6: Yarn over, knit 2 together, knit 13.

Row 7: Knit 3, [yarn over, knit 2 together] 3 times, knit 2, yarn over, knit 2 together, yarn over, knit 2. (16 stitches)

Techniques
Binding off–BO (page 14)
Blocking (page 27)
Casting on–CO (page 9)
Knit in front and back of same stitch–k1f&b (page 18)
Knit 2 together–k2tog (page 19)
Purl 2 together–p2tog (page 19)
Slip slip knit decrease–ssk (page 19)
Weaving in yarn tails (page 25)
Yarn over–yo (page 17)

Row 8: Yarn over, knit 2 together, knit 14.

Row 9: Knit 3, [knit 2 together, yarn over] 2 times, knit 2, knit 2 together, [yarn over, knit 2 together] 2 times, knit 1. (15 stitches)

Row 10: Yarn over, knit 2 together, knit 13.

Row 11: Knit 2, [knit 2 together, yarn over] 2 times, knit 2, knit 2 together, [yarn over, knit 2 together] 2 times, knit 1. (14 stitches)

Row 12: Yarn over, knit 2 together, knit 12.

Row 13: Knit 3, knit 2 together, yarn over, knit 2, knit 2 together, [yarn over, knit 2 together] 2 times, knit 1. (13 stitches)

Row 14: Yarn over, knit 2 together, knit 11.

Row 15: Knit 2, knit 2 together, yarn over, knit 2, knit 2 together, [yarn over, knit 2 together] 2 times, knit 1. (12 stitches)

Row 16: Yarn over, knit 2 together, knit 10.

Repeat rows 1–16 for pattern. Continue in pattern until the piece, when slightly stretched, fits across bottom edge of towel.

Complete edging, working row 16 of pattern repeat as follows: Yarn over, knit 2 together, bind off 1 stitch (this will be the yarn over the stitch remaining from the decrease), *knit 1, bind off 1 stitch**. Repeat from * to ** to end of row. See Finishing, below.

Sage-color edging on sage towel

Cast on 8 stitches.

Row 1: Knit 5, yarn over, knit 1, yarn over, knit 2. (10 stitches)

Row 2: Purl 6, increase in next stitch by knitting into front and back loops, knit 3. (11 stitches)

Row 3: Knit 4, purl 1, knit 2, yarn over, knit 1, yarn over, knit 3. (13 stitches)

Row 4: Purl 8, knit 1 front and back, knit 4. (14 stitches)

Row 5: Knit 4, purl 2, knit 3, yarn over, knit 1, yarn over, knit 4. (16 stitches)

Row 6: Purl 10, knit 1 front and back, knit 5. (17 stitches)

Row 7: Knit 4, purl 3, knit 4, yarn over, knit 1, yarn over, knit 5. (19 stitches)

Row 8: Purl 12, knit 1 front and back, knit 6. (20 stitches)

Row 9: Knit 4, purl 4, slip slip knit, knit 7, knit 2 together, knit 1. (18 stitches)

Row 10: Purl 10, knit 1 front and back, knit 7. (19 stitches)

Row 11: Knit 4, purl 5, slip slip knit, knit 5, knit 2 together, knit 1. (17 stitches)

Row 12: Purl 8, knit 1 front and back, knit 2, purl 1, knit 5. (18 stitches)

Row 13: Knit 4, purl 1, knit 1, purl 4, slip slip knit, knit 3, knit 2 together, knit 1. (16 stitches)

Row 14: Purl 6, knit 1 front and back, knit 3, purl 1, knit 5. (17 stitches)

Row 15: Knit 4, purl 1, knit 1, purl 5, slip slip knit, knit 1, knit 2 together, knit 1. (15 stitches)

Row 16: Purl 4, knit 1 front and back, knit 4, purl 1, knit 5. (16 stitches)

Row 17: Knit 4, purl 1, knit 1, purl 6, slip 1 knitwise, knit 2 together, pass slipped stitch over, knit 1. (14 stitches)

Row 18: Purl 2 together, bind off 5 stitches, purl 3, knit 4. (8 stitches)

Repeat row 1–18 for pattern. Work in pattern until the piece, when slightly stretched, fits across bottom edge of towel. Complete edging, binding off all stitches in pattern at row 18. See Finishing, below.

Finishing

Weave in all yarn tails to wrong side of work. Block. Pin edging to 1 end of towel; thread sewing needle with matching thread, and attach edging to towel with overcast stitch. Remove all pins.

Curly Striped Pillow

This multicolor pillow is made in two pieces, with a flap on one side that folds over to form a buttonhole closure. To add extra character, the curly, thick yarn is woven, not knit, between the stitches.

Designer: Judy Dercum

Techniques
Backstitch (page 23)
Binding off—BO (page 14)
Blocking (page 27)
Cable cast-on (page 9)
Casting on—CO (page 9)
Garter stitch (page 15)
Stranding yarn (page 20)
Weaving in yarn tails (page 25)

Size
18×18″ (46×46cm)
with side 1 flap folded

❀ ❀ ❀

Gauge
12 stitches/20 rows=4″ (10cm)
using 2 strands worsted weight
yarn in garter stitch

❀ ❀ ❀

What You'll Need
Yarn: 800 yards [732m]/16oz [454g]
worsted weight wool yarn (100%
wool): 8oz (226g) color A and color C;
4 oz (102g) colors B, D, and E;
30 yards [28m]/16oz [454g] Thick
Spun, a specialty handspun yarn
(100% wool): 8 yards [7.4m] color
C-THICK
We used: La Lana Wools Millspun
Knitting Worsted (100% wool):
Lavender (yarn A), 2 skeins;
Madder—pale (yarn B), 1 skein; Indian
Paint Brush—light (yarn C), 2 skeins;
Brazilwood III (yarn D), 1 skein; Apple-
Green (yarn E), 1 skein. La Lana Wools
Thick Spun (100% handspun, super
bulky-weight wool): Indian Paint Brush
(yarn C-THICK), 8 yards

Needles: US size 10 (6mm)
circular 24″ (61cm) long or
14″ (35.5cm) straight

Notions: Safety pin; stitch markers;
tapestry needle; sewing needle and
thread to match; five 1¼″ (3.2cm)
buttons; 16×16″ (40.5×40.5cm)
pillow form

Make side 1 (back)

Holding 2 strands of yarn A together as 1, cast on 57 stitches. Work 8 rows in garter stitch. Cut yarn, leaving 4″ (10cm) tails. (Leave a 4″ [10cm] yarn tail each time you change yarns, except with C-THICK; follow the instructions below for this yarn.)

Change to yarn B, and holding 2 strands together as 1, work 2 rows in garter stitch.

Begin Stranded Thick Spun pattern (worked over garter stitch)
Row 1: (right side) With 2 strands yarn C, knit all stitches. Place a safety pin on this side to mark it as right side of work.
Row 2: (wrong side) Knit.
Row 3: (right side) With 2 strands yarn C, knit 1; with 1 strand C-THICK and leaving a 1″ (2.5cm) tail on wrong side of work, *bring C-THICK yarn forward from wrong side to right side, traveling between the last stitch worked on the right needle and the first stitch on the left needle. Drop C-THICK in front and leave it there; don't cut yarn. With 2 strands yarn C, knit next 3 stitches. Pick up C-THICK and strand across the 3 stitches just worked on the right side; take yarn to wrong side of work, traveling between stitches on right and left needles. Drop C-THICK in back and leave it there. Using 2 strands yarn C, knit 1**. Repeat from * to ** across row (ending with C-THICK on wrong side of work). Using 2 strands yarn C, knit remaining stitch.
Row 4: With 2 strands yarn C, knit.

Pillow back

Row 5: With 2 strands yarn C, knit.

Row 6: (wrong side) *With 2 strands yarn C, knit 1; bring 1 strand C-THICK up from row 3 and take it to right side of work, traveling between stitches on right and left needles. Drop C-THICK on right side of work and leave it there. With 2 strands yarn C, knit 1. Strand C-THICK across the right side of the 3 stitches just worked and then return C-THICK to wrong side, traveling between the right and left needles. Drop C-THICK on wrong side and leave it there**. Repeat from * to ** across row. With 2 strands yarn C, knit remaining stitch.

Row 7: Knit.

Row 8: Knit.

Row 9: (right side) Repeat row 3. Cut C-THICK, leaving 1″ (2.5cm) tail to weave in later.

Row 10: (wrong side) Knit. Cut yarn C, leaving about 4″ (10cm) tails to weave in later.

Begin Woven Stitch pattern: Change to yarn D, and work as follows:

Row 1: (right side) *Knit 1, slip 1 with yarn in front**; repeat from * to ** across row to last stitch, end with knit 1.

Row 2: (wrong side) Purl.

Row 3: Knit 1, *knit 1, slip 1 with yarn in front**; repeat from * to ** across row, end with knit 2.

Row 4: Purl.

Work 3 repeats of Woven Stitch pattern (12 rows). Change to yarn E, knit 4 rows. Change to yarn A, knit 10 rows. Change to yarn B, knit 4 rows. Change to yarn C and C-THICK, and work 10 rows in Stranded Thick Spun pattern. Change to yarn D, work 4 rows in Woven Stitch pattern. Change to yarn E, knit 4 rows. Change to yarn A, knit 8 rows.

Next row: (right side) Continuing with yarn A, purl across row to form turn line for flap. Knit 8 rows.

Next row: (wrong side) Knit across row, placing stitch markers before stitches 6, 17, 28, 39, and 50 to mark for buttonhole placements.

Buttonholes

Next row: (right side) Make a 2-stitch, 1-row buttonhole at each marker as follows: Knit up to (but not including) the first marked stitch, then bring yarn between needles to front of work, slip next stitch (the marked stitch) from left needle to right needle, take yarn between needles to back of work and drop it. *Slip next stitch from left needle onto right needle, then pass second stitch on right needle (counting from needle tip back) over first stitch and drop it off the needle (the same as binding off). Repeat from * once more (2 stitches are bound off). Return the last slipped stitch to left needle, and turn work to wrong side. With yarn in back, cable cast-on 3 stitches (1 more stitch than you bound off). Turn work back to right side. With yarn in back, slip first stitch from left needle to right needle, then pass the extra cable cast-on stitch over the slipped stitch to close buttonhole. Knit to next marked stitch, and make another buttonhole in same way. Repeat, making a buttonhole at each marked stitch, then knit to end of row.

Next row: (wrong side) Knit.

Next row: Bind off all stitches. Cut yarn, and thread 4″ (10cm) yarn tail on tapestry needle. Weave across stitches on wrong side to secure. Repeat with each yarn tail except C-THICK. With sewing needle and thread, tack down C-THICK ends on wrong side of work.

Make side 2 (front)

Holding 2 strands of yarn A together as 1, cast on 57 stitches. Work 4 rows in garter stitch. Cut yarn, leaving 4″ (10cm) tail as in side 1. Change to yarn B, and work 2 rows of garter stitch.

Side 2 Stranded Thick Spun pattern

Row 1: (right side) With yarn C, knit across row. Place a safety pin on this side to mark it as right side of work.

Row 2: (wrong side) Knit.

Row 3: (right side) Knit 1, leaving a 1″ (2.5cm) C-THICK tail on wrong side. *Bring yarn forward from wrong side between last stitch worked on right needle and first stitch on left needle. Drop C-THICK. With yarn C, knit 3 stitches. Pick up C-THICK and strand across the right side of 3 stitches just worked. Move C-THICK to wrong side of work, traveling between stitches on right and left needles, and leave it there. With yarn C, knit 1 stitch**. Repeat from * to ** across row (ending with C-THICK on wrong side of work). With yarn C, knit remaining stitch.

Row 4: Knit.

Row 5: Knit.

Row 6: (wrong side) *With 2 strands of yarn C, knit 1, bring C-THICK up from row 3 on wrong side and take it to right side of work, traveling between stitches on right and left needles. Drop C-THICK on right side. With yarn C, knit 3 stitches. Strand C-THICK across right side of 3 stitches just worked and then return it to wrong side, traveling between right and left needles. Drop C-THICK**. Repeat from * to ** across row. With yarn C, knit remaining stitch. Cut C-THICK, leaving 1″ (2.5cm) tail.

Change to yarn D, and work 4 rows of Woven Stitch pattern. Change to yarn E, and work 2 rows in garter stitch. Work the following stitch patterns and colors as follows: *With yarn A, work 4 rows in garter stitch; with yarn B, work 2 rows in garter stitch; with yarn C and C-THICK, work 6 rows of Stranded Thick Spun pattern; with yarn D, work 4 rows in Woven Stitch pattern; and with yarn E, work 2 rows in garter stitch**. Repeat from * to ** 3 more times (72 rows total).

With yarn E, work 6 rows in garter stitch. Bind off all stitches. Weave in all loose ends, and tack down C-THICK tails to wrong side of work as in side 1.

Finishing

Block both sides to measurements, with side 1 flap folded over to wrong side. Using threaded tapestry needle, with right sides together and wrong sides facing out, sew around both sides and bottom edge with backstitch. Leave the side 1 flap edges open. Turn work to right side and fold flap edges down over the outside of side 2 to form closure. Sew buttons to side 2 opposite buttonhole openings. Insert pillow form, and button the flap closed.

What a Novelty!

There's never been a better time to be a knitter. And that's because there's never been so many wonderful yarns available. Knitters are no longer limited to wool in whatever shades they can dye themselves— they can now buy wool in all the colors of the rainbow. Also available is a mind-boggling assortment of novelty yarns, including light and fuzzy mohair, bumpy bouclé, soft chenille, satiny ribbon, tweeds flecked with spots of color, cool cottons, and blends of every fiber imaginable. Working with some of these yarns may take a little getting used to, but they are perfect for the beginning knitter since they show off best in simple stitch patterns. With these yarns, even stockinette stitch can be a showstopper.

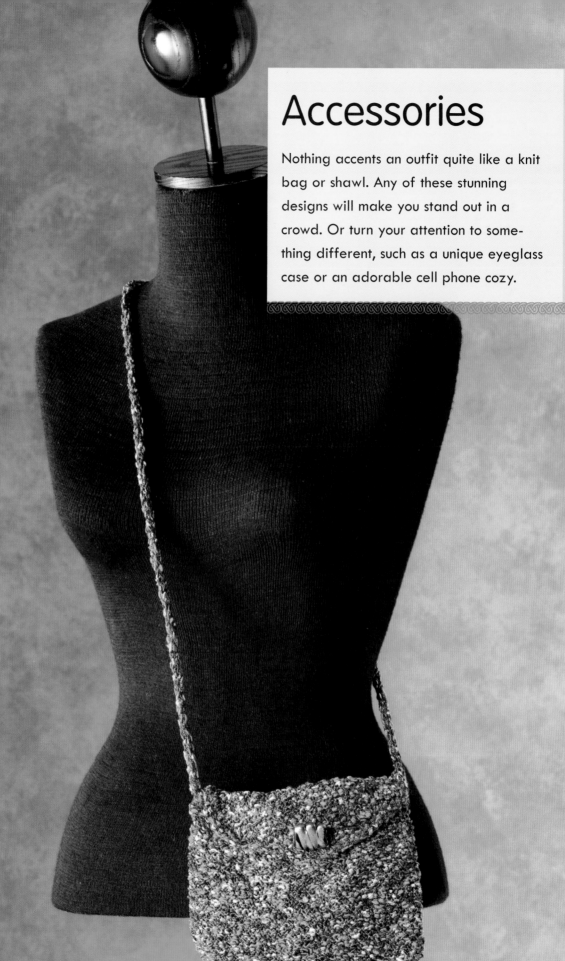

Accessories

Nothing accents an outfit quite like a knit bag or shawl. Any of these stunning designs will make you stand out in a crowd. Or turn your attention to something different, such as a unique eyeglass case or an adorable cell phone cozy.

Textured Shawl

A showstopper in glorious shades of red and seemingly endless textures, this shawl is sure to take your breath away. And who would ever dream that a shawl this gorgeous could be so easy to knit?

Designer: Lisa Daniels

Techniques
Binding off–BO (page 14)
Casting on–CO (page 9)
Knit stitch–k (page 12)
Purl stitch–p (page 13)

Size
16×80″ (40.5×203cm)
in length, plus fringe

❀ ❀ ❀

Gauge
14 stitches=6″ (15cm)

❀ ❀ ❀

What You'll Need

Yarn: 4oz (114g) mohair; 4oz (114g) merino ribbon; 4oz (114g) mohair and nylon blend; 8oz (227g) kid mohair and nylon blend; 8oz (227g) mohair and wool blend

We used: Mountain Colors Mohair (78% mohair, 13% wool, 9% nylon): ruby river (yarn A), 1 skein; Mountain Colors Merino Ribbon (80% kid mohair, 20% nylon): ruby river (yarn B), 1 skein; Mountain Colors Moguls (96% mohair, 4% nylon): ruby river (yarn C), 2 skeins; Mountain Colors Mountain Goat (55% mohair, 45% wool): ruby river (yarn D), 2 skeins; Mountain Colors Wooly Feathers (65% kid mohair, 35% nylon): ruby river (yarn E), 1 skein

Needles: US size 11 (8mm) circular 32″ (81.5cm) long

Pattern
Row 1: Purl.
Rows 2 and 3: Knit.
Row 4: Purl.
Repeat 4 rows for pattern.

Notes:
• As you work the shawl, cut the yarn at the beginning and end of each row, leaving 18″ (46cm) tails at both ends. This creates the fringe and eliminates the need to weave in the yarn tails.
• When working with yarn D, use 2 strands held together as 1.
• The cast-on stitches are the width of the shawl.

Make the shawl

Using 2 strands of yarn D held together as 1, cast on 150 stitches, leaving 18″ (46cm) tails. Knit 1 row, purl 1 row. Join yarn E, and work 4 rows in pattern.

*With yarn B, work 4 rows in pattern. With yarn C, work 4 rows in pattern. With yarn A, work 4 rows in pattern. With yarn D (using 2 strands held together as 1), work 4 rows in pattern**. Repeat the 16 rows from * to **. (38 rows from cast-on edge)

Continue work as follows:

With yarn E, work 4 rows in pattern. *With yarn B, work 4 rows in pattern. With yarn C, work 4 rows in pattern. With yarn A, work 4 rows in pattern. With yarn D (using 2 strands held together as 1), work 4 rows in pattern**. Repeat the 16 rows from * to ** (74 rows from cast-on edge). With yarn B, work 4 rows in pattern. With yarn C, work 4 rows in pattern. With yarn A, work 4 rows in pattern. With yarn E, work 4 rows in pattern.

End shawl working rows 1 and 2 of pattern with yarn D (using 2 strands held together as 1). (92 rows from cast-on edge)

Bind off loosely with yarn D.

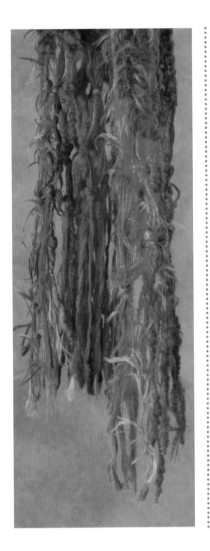

Finishing

Beginning at left edge of row, allow the first fringe tail to hang straight until later. *Tie next 2 fringe tails into an overhand knot about 3″ (7.5cm) from knitted side edge; repeat from * across all strands, leaving the last strand hanging straight. Begin at left edge again, and tie first and second yarn tails into overhand knot about 3″ (7.5cm) from first row of knots. **Tie next 2 strands into overhand knot 3″ (7.5cm) from first row of knots; repeat from ** across row to end. Repeat fringe on other short side of shawl. *Optional:* Using the same strands as first row of knots, make a third row of knots 3″ (7.5cm) down from last row of knots.

The Knitty-Gritty

Swatch What I Can Do!

As a knitter, whether novice or experienced or somewhere in between, no doubt you're familiar with the feeling that comes when you finish a project and are left with some extra yarn. The problem is, it almost never seems to be enough yarn to complete another project. It seems a shame to let the yarn go to waste, but what can you do with all of these scraps?

It's easy to turn them into a keepsake quilt, a sachet, a scarf, or a pillow. Knit simple swatches from your leftover yarn, arrange the swatches in an interesting pattern, and then sew them together. If needed, you can pick up stitches and knit a little here and there to fill in the edges. No perfection needed here.... All that counts is fun, imagination, and treasuring your memories!

Cell Phone Cozies

Keep your cell phone in good shape while giving it a unique look with these knitted cozies. We've included patterns for two popular cell phone models—a flip phone and one with a display window.

Designer: Lucie Sinkler

Techniques

Backstitch (page 23)
Binding off—BO (page 14)
Casting on—CO (page 9)
Knit 2 together—k2tog (page 19)
Mattress stitch (page 23)
Stockinette stitch—St st (page 15)
Weaving in yarn tails (page 25)

Size

Blue cozy: 2½×3″ (6.5×7.5cm)
Pink cozy: 2¾×3¾″ (7×9.5 cm)

⊗ ⊗ ⊗

Gauge

14 stitches=4″ (10cm)

⊗ ⊗ ⊗

What You'll Need

Yarn: 30 yards (27m) boucle
yarn for each cozy
We used: The Plymouth Italian Collection
Firenze Boucle (30% wool, 30%
acrylic, 40% nylon): #442 pink, 1 skein
(for pink cozy); #418 blue, 1 skein (for
blue cozy)

Needles: US size 7 (4½mm)

Notions: Tapestry needle; ⅝″ (1.5cm)
button (for blue cozy); long sewing pins
with large colored heads; sewing
needle and thread to match; 2 stitch
holders; ½″ (1.3cm) snap
(for pink cozy)

Note: Because different models of cell
phones have different measurements,
adjust the stitch counts accordingly.
Use your gauge as a guide.

Make the blue cozy

Cast on 8 stitches. Work in stockinette stitch for 7″ (18cm).
End with knit row.

Shape the flap
Row 1: Bind off 1 stitch (space for antenna), purl to end. (7 stitches)
Row 2: Knit.
Rows 3, 5, 7, and 9: Purl.
Row 4: Knit 4, knit 2 together, knit 1. (6 stitches)
Row 6: Knit 3, knit 2 together, knit 1. (5 stitches)
Row 8: Knit 2, knit 2 together, knit 1. (4 stitches)
Row 10: Knit 1, knit 2 together, knit 1. (3 stitches)
Bind off all stitches.

Make buttonhole loop: Cut yarn about 18″ (46cm) from last stitch;
thread on tapestry needle. Insert needle into beginning stitch of bind-off
row and carry the yarn to end stitch of bind-off row (other side of flap),
leaving a big-enough loop for button to fit through. Wrap yarn around
loop several times to strengthen, and secure yarn by backstitching several
times on wrong side of work.

Finishing

Fold piece in half with right sides together to form the cell phone pocket
(don't include the flap). Pin side edges together. With sewing needle and
matching thread, whipstitch side seams closed. Remove pins.

Make the handle: Cut length of yarn about 36″ (90cm) long. Thread
tapestry needle and secure 1 end of yarn on inside of side seam, under
the top edge. Insert needle through side seam on opposite side, under the
top edge, leaving a loop about 13″ (33cm) long. Wrap yarn around loop
several times to make a stronger handle, then return needle to first seam
and secure end by weaving through side seam on wrong side of work.
Turn piece to right side.

Attach the button: Fold flap over top edge of pocket, and match loop
with the place to attach button. With sewing needle and thread, stitch
button in place. Weave in ends to wrong side of work; secure firmly.

Make the pink cozy

Cast on 11 stitches. Work in stockinette stitch for 7½″ (19cm). End with
purl row.

Make the display window: Knit 3 stitches, bind off 5 stitches, knit to
end. (3 stitches on each side of bind-off). Place first set of stitches on
holder. Work stockinette stitch over remaining 3 stitches for 1″ (2.5cm);

end with purl row. Cut yarn, leaving 6″ (15cm) tail to secure later. Place stitches on second holder. Slip stitches from first holder onto needle. With wrong side facing, rejoin yarn at beginning of bound-off stitches. Purl 3 stitches. Work even in stockinette stitch for 1″ (2.5cm).

Next row: Knit. At end of row, cast on 5 stitches using either knitted cast-on or cable cast-on. Knit stitches from second holder (11 stitches). Work in stockinette stitch for 1″ (2.5cm). End with purl row.

Make the strap

Next row: (right side) Bind off 3 stitches, knit to end of row. (8 stitches)

Next row: (wrong side) Bind off 4 stitches, purl to end of row. (4 stitches)

Continue working strap on 4 stitches for a total of 5″ (12.5cm). Bind off all stitches.

Finishing

With right sides together, fold cozy in half (don't include strap). Pin side edges together. With sewing needle and thread, whipstitch side seams together. Remove all pins. Turn piece to right side. Sew 1 side of snap on wrong side of strap, about ½″ (1.3cm) from end. Fold strap in half and, on back side of cozy, mark where to attach other half of snap. Sew snap in place. Weave all yarn ends to wrong side, and secure.

The Knitty-Gritty

A Gift of Knitting

Show off your new talent by giving a hand-knit gift. Not only will you feel proud, the recipient will treasure the gift as something truly special, knowing it came from the heart. Be creative with your gift giving! You might knit a new mother a darling layette for her baby. Honor a special anniversary or a grandparent's birthday by creating an afghan of simple stockinette-stitch squares—ask each of the grandchildren or family members to dip their hand in fabric paint and stamp their handprint onto a square. Buy your teenager a cell phone for safety and for your peace of mind, and knit a trendy phone cozy for her to carry it in. Each time she sees it, she'll remember you're only a phone call away.

Eyeglass Case

Eyeglasses will be well protected in this densely knit case. Choose a multicolor yarn to display the subtle texture of linen stitch. The whole case is worked as one piece, which makes it a perfect project for a beginner.

Designer: Lucie Sinkler

Techniques

Binding off—BO (page 14)
Cable cast-on (page 9)
Casting on—CO (page 9)
Knitted cast-on (page 11)
Mattress stitch—(page 23)
Slip stitch purlwise (page 17)

Size

3½×7½" (9×19cm)

⊗ ⊗ ⊗

Gauge

26 stitches/40 rows=4"
(10cm) in pattern

⊗ ⊗ ⊗

What You'll Need

Yarn: 100 yards heavy worsted weight cotton
We used: Plymouth Fantasy Naturale (100% cotton): #9709 multicolor in blues, greens, and purple, 1 skein

Needles: US size 8 (5mm)

Notions: ⅞" (2.2cm) button; scissors; tapestry needle; sewing needle and thread to match (if buttonholes are too small to use yarn)

Make the case

Cast on 49 stitches.

Row 1: (right side) Knit 1, *bring yarn to front of work (as if to purl), slip next stitch purlwise, take yarn to back of work, knit 1**; repeat from * to ** to end of row.

Row 2: (wrong side) Purl 2, *take yarn to back, slip 1 purlwise, bring yarn forward, purl 1**; repeat from * to ** to last stitch, end with purl 1. Repeat rows 1 and 2 for pattern. Work pattern until piece measures 7½" (19cm) in length, ending with wrong-side row.

Next row: (right side) Bind off 26 stitches at beginning of row, work remaining stitches in pattern. (23 stitches)

Next row: (wrong side) Bind off first 2 stitches, work remaining stitches in pattern. (21 stitches)

Make flap: Work in pattern on remaining 21 stitches for 1¾" (4.5cm). End with wrong-side row.

Make buttonhole: Work 8 stitches in pattern, bind off center 5 stitches for buttonhole, work remaining stitches in pattern.

Next row: (wrong side) Work in pattern up to bound-off stitches, cast on 5 stitches using knitted cast-on or cable cast-on. Finish row in pattern. Work even in established pattern for ¾" (2cm) more from buttonhole; bind off all stitches.

Finishing

Fold piece in half lengthwise, leaving flap free. With tapestry needle and yarn, sew together bottom and side seams using mattress stitch. Fold flap over opening; sew button in place. Weave yarn ends to wrong side and secure.

Oops!

Loosen Up!

A bound-off edge needs to be as elastic as the rest of the knitted piece. If you are having trouble keeping your edges loose enough, try using a needle up to three sizes larger than what you used for the rest of the piece to work the stitches off the needle.

Felted Market Bags

A hand-knit market bag is just the thing for a trip to the neighborhood farmers' market. Both the large tote and the smaller bag make a statement with bold stripes; the smaller bag goes a step further by incorporating the fashionable "tweed" look. Designer: Lucie Sinkler

Size

Large bag: (before felting) 17" (43cm) wide, 16" (40.5cm) deep, handle 29½" (75cm) long; (after felting) 15½" (39.5cm) wide, 12" (30.5cm) deep, handle 26" (66cm) long

Small bag: (before felting) 15" (38cm) wide, 9" (23cm) deep, handle 14" (35.5cm) long; (after felting) 14" (35.5cm) wide, 7½" (19cm) deep, handle 12½" (31.5cm) long

❀ ❀ ❀

Gauge

Before felting: 12½ stitches/20 rows=4" (10cm)

❀ ❀ ❀

What You'll Need

Yarn: Large bag: 100% medium weight wool yarn: 600 yards (549m) color A; 400 yards (366m) color B. Small bag: 100% medium weight wool yarn: 150 yards (137m) color A and color B
Superwash wool or synthetics will not felt; do not use for felting projects.
We used: Cascade Yarns Cascade 220: #8555 black (yarn A), 3 balls for large bag, 2 balls for small bag; #8021 natural (yarn B), 2 balls for large bag, 2 balls for small bag

Needles: US size 10½ (6.5mm) circular 24" (61cm) long

Notions: 3 stitch holders; stitch markers; tapestry needle

Miscellaneous: Washing machine, laundry detergent, pillowcase or lingerie bag

Notes: Instructions are written for large bag; numbers for small bag are in brackets.

All pieces are worked holding 2 strands of yarn together.

⋯⋯⋯⋯⋯⋯⋯⋯⋯⋯⋯⋯⋯⋯⋯⋯⋯

Make the handles

Holding 2 strands of color A together as 1, cast on 10 stitches. Work in stockinette stitch for 64 [30] rows. Cut yarn, leaving a 4" (10cm) tail; slip stitches onto holder. Pick up 10 stitches at cast-on edge, and work in stockinette stitch for 64 [30] rows. Cut yarn, leaving a 4" (10cm) tail; slip stitches onto another holder.

Repeat to make the second handle, except do not cut the yarn in the last step. Leave those stitches on needle. You will have 2 knitted strips with live stitches on both sides.

Make the bag body

Attach the handle: (see fig. A, page 60) Using the second handle with 10 stitches and the working yarn (color A) attached, use the cable cast-on method to cast on 10 [8] stitches in front of the stitches on the needle. (20 [18] stitches)

Fold the knit strip in half to create the handle. Transfer 10 stitches from stitch holder onto working needle; knit across these stitches (30 [28] stitches). Cast on 26 [22] stitches using the cable cast-on method, and then knit across 10 stitches from first handle (66 [56] stitches). Cast on 10 [8] stitches in front of these stitches, knit across second set of 10 stitches from first handle, and then cast on 26 [22] stitches using the cable cast-on (112 [100] stitches). Join work into a circle, taking care not to twist stitches. Place stitch marker in front of first stitch worked to indicate beginning of round.

Rounds 1, 3, 5, and 7: Purl.

Rounds 2, 4, 6, and 8: Knit.

Round 9: Knit until 13 [11] stitches before the marker. Place second stitch marker (use another color to distinguish from first marker). The

second marker will indicate beginning of round for color changes. Cut yarn, leaving 4″ (10cm) tail to weave in later.

Create color sequence: For large bag, work [9 rounds color B, 9 rounds color A] 4 times (72 rounds). For small bag, holding 1 strand color A and 1 strand color B together as 1, knit 11 rounds. With 2 strands color B held together as 1, knit 11 rounds. Change to 1 strand A and 1 strand B held together, and knit 11 rounds. Using 2 strands B, knit 4 rounds.

Make the bag base

Knit 8 [8] stitches past second marker, then bind off 40 [34] stitches. Knit across next 16 stitches, place them on holder, bind off 40 [34] stitches, then knit across 16 stitches remaining on needle. Work 35 [27] rows in stockinette stitch. Bind off.

Place stitches from holder back on needle, and rejoin yarn. Work 36 [28] rows in stockinette stitch. Bind off.

Finishing

Thread tapestry needle with 18″ (46cm) strand of yarn, and seam center of base together using mattress stitch. Rethread yarn as necessary. Starting in middle of bag base, whipstitch bound-off edges from bag

body to base sides. Base piece will be slightly longer and will need to be eased to the sides (knitted fabric shrinks more lengthwise). Weave in all loose ends to wrong side of bag.

Follow felting instructions on page 27.

Tote It Your Way

Somewhere between the plastic shopping bag in which you brought your yarn home and an expensive craft box or tote bag, there's a whole range of great ways to get your yarn from one place to another.

Try an oversize handbag, a backpack, or a wicker basket. Or how about shopping in the hardware store for a tool "apron" with pockets that hang over a five-gallon bucket? You can store yarn in the bucket, put needles and gadgets in the pockets, and even use the bucket as a seat when you want your knitting to be portable.

Of course, there's always the opportunity to design and knit a bag just like either of these in your favorite colors, adding pockets and embellishments to make it uniquely your own. You may want to add lining to the inside so needles don't slip out!

Fig. A

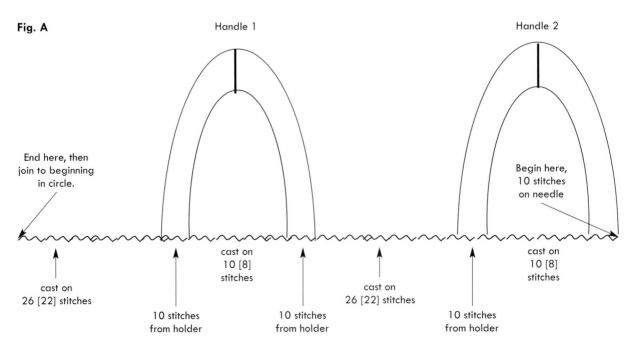

Beaded Wedding Purses

With the elegant look of days gone by, a knitted wedding purse will delight your favorite bride on her special day. Both the modern and the traditional versions are sure to become treasured heirlooms.

Designer: Beth Walker O'Brien

Techniques

Binding off–BO (page 14)

Kitchener stitch (page 24)

Knit in front and back of same stitch–k1f&b (page 18)

Long tail cast-on (page 10)

Make 1 increase–m1 (page 18)

Mattress stitch (page 23)

Size

(Both bags) Approximately 7×6"
(18×15cm) not including fringe
and loops

Gauge

22 stitches/36 rows=4" (10cm)
in diagonal bead stitch pattern

What You'll Need

Yarn: 246 yards mercerized cotton sport weight yarn (123 yards [112m]/50g)

We used: Reynolds Yarns Saucy Sport (100% mercerized cotton): #809 eggshell, 2 balls

Beads: 1,900 size 6° (4mm) seed beads (for each purse); 45 size 11° (2.1mm) seed beads (modern version only)

We used: 10 strings of size 6° (4mm) seed beads (190 beads per string): pearl eggshell, for each purse. Additionally, the modern version purse requires 45 size 11° seed beads

Needles: US size 2 (2.75mm), US size 3 (3.25mm)

Notions: Stitch holder; tapestry needle; sewing needle (size 6° seed bead must fit over eye of needle) and thread to match; beading needle; size D Nymo thread; 1 yard (91.5cm) silk ribbon, ⅞" (2.2cm) wide

---

Diagonal Bead Stitch pattern

Row 1: (right side) Knit 1, [knit 1 bead, knit 2] 14 times, knit 1.

Row 2 and all even-numbered rows: Purl.

Row 3: Knit 2, [knit 1 bead, knit 2] 14 times.

Row 5: Knit 3, [knit 1 bead, knit 2] 13 times, knit 1 bead, knit 1.

Row 6: Purl.

Stringing beads onto knitting yarn

• To **knit 1 bead**, insert right-hand needle into the stitch on the left needle as you normally would. Slide a bead up the yarn, and as you wrap the yarn and pull it through the stitch on the left needle, pull the bead through with the yarn.

• To **slip 1 bead**, slide bead up to needles, and knit next stitch. Bead is anchored between 2 knitted stitches.

Tie overhand knot in bead string.

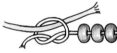
Insert yarn end, then tighten knot.

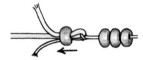
Slide bead from string onto yarn.

Note: Pattern instructions are provided for both the traditional and modern versions of the purse. Instructions apply to both versions unless otherwise noted.

Make the purse

Transfer 4 strings of beads onto yarn. Using size 2 needles and long tail cast-on method, cast on 38 stitches as follows: Place slipknot on needle, [slip 1 bead, cast on 1 stitch] 37 times. It's important that the yarn with the beads is over your forefinger when casting on so beads will lie to back of needle.

Row 1: (right side) Knit.

Row 2: (wrong side) Knit 1, [slip 1 bead, knit 1] 37 times.

Rows 3–10: Repeat rows 1 and 2 four more times. From right side, there should be 6 rows of beads.

Row 11: Knit.

Change to size 3 needles.

Traditional version only:

Row 12: Purl 4, yarn over, [purl 6, yarn over] 5 times, purl 4. (44 stitches)

Modern version only:

Row 12: Purl 4, make 1, [purl 6, make 1] 5 times, purl 4. (44 stitches)

Both versions:

Work 9 repeats of Diagonal Bead Stitch pattern (54 rows). *Do not bind off.* Place stitches on holder.

Repeat for second side of purse.

Finishing

With right sides facing, seam bottom edges of purse together using Kitchener stitch. Turn right side out.

Make beaded loops (traditional version only):
Embellish bottom of purse with 13 beaded loops, each loop containing 24 beads (see photo). To make the loops, thread sharp-pointed sewing needle with Nymo thread. Starting at 1 end of purse, securely attach thread to inside of purse, and push needle through to outside of purse. Slide 24 beads onto thread, pushing them securely against bottom of purse. *Insert needle back through to inside of purse approximately ¾″ from beginning of loop. Bring needle back to outside of purse in the center of the previously created loop, and slide 24 more beads onto thread**. Repeat from * to ** along bottom of purse.

Make beaded fringe (modern version only): Embellish bottom of purse with about 42 strands of beaded fringe, each strand containing 11 size 6° seed beads, with 1 size 11° seed bead used to anchor larger beads. To make the fringe, thread sharp-pointed sewing needle with Nymo thread. Starting at 1 end of purse, securely attach thread to inside of purse, and push needle through to outside of purse. *Slide 11 of the larger seed beads (size 6°) onto thread, followed by 1 small seed bead (size 11°). Skipping the small seed bead, push needle back through the 11 larger seed beads to inside of purse, pulling thread so beads are secure against bottom of purse. Pull needle back through to outside of purse right next to previous strand of fringe**. Repeat from * to ** along bottom of purse.

Both versions: With yarn threaded on tapestry needle, use mattress stitch to sew side seams together. Weave in all remaining ends to wrong side.

Make beaded straps (traditional version only): Sew satin ribbon to inside edge at top of purse (right above eyelets) with sewing needle and matching thread. Fold bottom edge of ribbon as you sew so as not to cover eyelets. Make 2 separate strings of beads, each 20″ (51cm) long, by transferring beads onto knitting yarn (see page 62). Thread beaded strands through eyelets at top of purse (fig. A, page 64). Securely knot ends of beaded strands together, making sure there are no gaps between beads. Arrange beaded strands so knots lie to inside of purse.

Make knitted strap (modern version only): Cast on 7 stitches. With yarn in front, slip 1 stitch purlwise, knit 6. With yarn in front, slip 1 stitch purlwise, slip 1 bead, knit 2 together, [slip 1 bead, knit 1] 4 times. (6 stitches)

Row 1: With yarn in front, slip 1 stitch purlwise, knit 5.

Row 2: With yarn in front, slip 1 stitch purlwise, [slip 1 bead, knit 1] 5 times. Repeat rows 1 and 2 for 7″ (18cm), ending with row 2.

Next row: With yarn in front, slip 1 stitch purlwise, knit into front and back loop of next stitch, knit 4. (7 stitches)

Bind off all stitches. Weave in ends to wrong side of strap. Sew satin ribbon on wrong side of strap with sewing needle and matching thread. Sew ends of strap to center front and center back of purse using tapestry needle threaded with knitting yarn. Sew satin ribbon to inside edge at top of purse.

Legacy in Lace

Start a new tradition or carry on an old one. If you knit with love and caring, you'll leave a legacy that will live on. A special heirloom afghan given to each new baby in your family to be passed down through the generations is one idea, or you might consider a special garter or Bible cover for a bride on her special day. It may be her "something new" and someday her daughter's "something old."

Fig. A—Traditional version

Threading first strap through eyelets

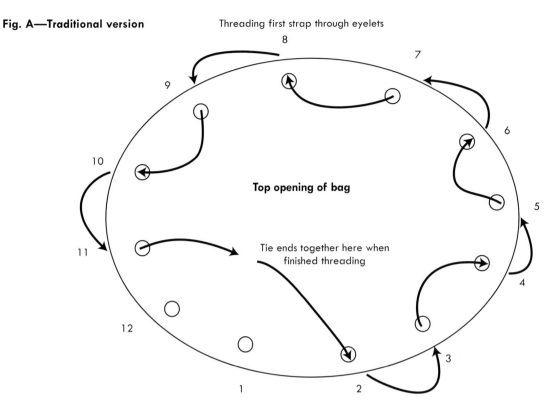

Top opening of bag

Tie ends together here when finished threading

Note: Side seams are between yarn overs 1 and 12 and yarn overs 6 and 7.

Threading second strap through eyelets

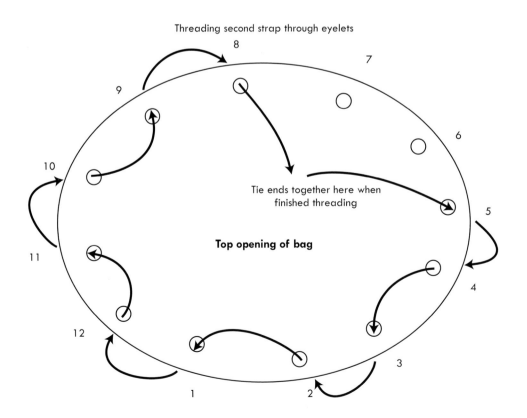

Tie ends together here when finished threading

Top opening of bag

Watercolor Wrap

The beauty of this shawl is not only in how it looks but in how relatively simple it is to make. The body uses simple increases and decreases to create a butterfly silhouette that gently hugs your shoulders as it drapes over your body.

Designer: Beth Walker O'Brien

Techniques

Decreases (page 19)

I-cord (page 21)

Increases (page 17)

Knit 2 together—k2tog (page 19)

Knitted cast-on (page 11)

Long tail cast-on (page 10)

Make 1 increase—m1 (page 18)

Slip slip knit decrease—ssk (page 19)

Yarn over—yo (page 17)

Size

29″ (73.5cm) in length, 62″ (157.5cm) in width (after blocking)

⊛　⊛　⊛

Gauge

16 stitches/36 rows=4″ (10cm) after blocking

⊛　⊛　⊛

What You'll Need

Yarn: 1,300 yards (1,189m) lace-weight yarn in variegated colors **We used:** Lorna's Laces Helen's Lace (50% silk, 50% wool): #18 watercolor, 1 hank

Needles: 2 US size 8 (5mm) circular, each 29″ (73.5cm) long; US size 9 (5.5mm) circular, 29″ (73.5cm)

Notions: Stitch markers; tapestry needle; rustproof pins for blocking

Make the wrap

With size 8 circular needles, *loosely* cast on 192 stitches using long tail cast-on method. Place marker between 87th and 88th stitches and another marker between 105th and 106th stitches.

Row 1: (wrong side) Knit.

Row 2: (right side) With yarn in front of work, slip 1, take yarn to back of work, slip slip knit decrease, knit to first marker, yarn over, slip marker, knit to second marker (18 stitches between markers), slip marker, yarn over, knit until 3 stitches remain in row, knit 2 together, knit 1.

Row 3: With yarn in front of work, slip 1, knit to end of row, slipping markers to maintain their place.

Repeat rows 2 and 3 for a total of 144 rows. You may adjust the length by working more or fewer rows at this time, but remember that the finished piece will be longer and wider after you block it. Cut yarn, leaving a 4″ (10cm) tail.

Make Old Shale lace border: Begin on left side of shawl, next to the cast-on edge (see fig. A). With other size 8 circular needles and right side facing, pick up 72 stitches, working into the slip-stitch selvedge edge (created in rows 2 and 3). Knit across 192 stitches on first needle, and pick up 72 stitches along left-hand side of shawl (336 stitches). Purl the next row.

Work Old Shale lace pattern, beginning with row 1 of chart. Note that a stitch is added at the beginning and end of every other row. When chart row 26 (wrong side) is finished, begin picot chain bind-off as follows.

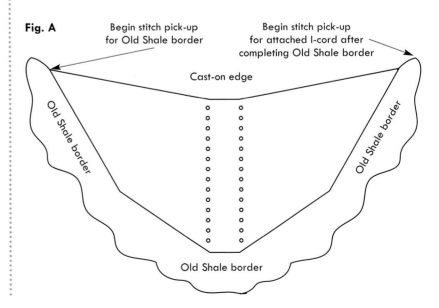

Fig. A

Picot chain bind-off

Step 1: (right side) Holding needle with stitches in left hand, cast 1 stitch on left-hand needle using knitted cast-on method.

Step 2: Knit 2 stitches (new cast-on stitch plus next stitch on left-hand needle).

Step 3: Insert tip of left-hand needle into second stitch on right-hand needle, and bind off 1 stitch.

Step 4: Knit 1 stitch, bind off 1 stitch. Slip remaining stitch from right-hand needle back to left-hand needle, making sure not to twist stitch.

Repeat steps 1–4 until all 336 stitches are bound off.

Attach I-cord edging: With size 9 circular needles, and beginning at right-side edge of cast-on (see fig. A), work I-cord edging along top of shawl. Use the following ratio when picking up stitches: Pick up 3 stitches for every 4 rows along top edge of Old Shale lace border, and pick up 1 stitch for every cast-on stitch across garter stitch portion. Cut yarn, leaving 4″ (10cm) tail. Thread tail on tapestry needle; weave through center of I-cord to secure.

Finishing

Weave in all loose ends to wrong side of work. Block shawl to size; let dry before unpinning.

They're Not Holes; It's Lace!

Lace patterns are made by working increases and decreases in each row. Because the number of increases does not always equal the number of decreases, the stitch count will not always remain the same on each row. However, most patterns will tell you which pattern rows you can use to check your stitch count.

Lace Chart

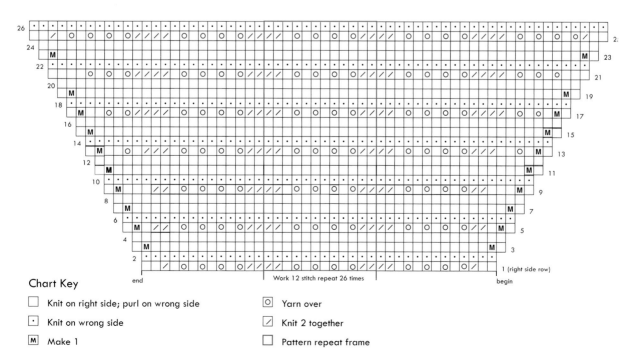

Chart Key

☐ Knit on right side; purl on wrong side	⊙ Yarn over
· Knit on wrong side	⁄ Knit 2 together
M Make 1	☐ Pattern repeat frame

Elegant Evening Bag

Glitzy yarn and a shimmery bead combine to make an elegant, eye-catching evening bag that's as nice as any sold in department stores. The bead is purely decorative; there are no buttonholes to make on this bag.

Designer: Adrienne Welch

Techniques

Cable cast-on (page 9)
I-cord (page 21)
Knit in front and back of same stitch—k1f&b (page 18)
Long tail cast-on (page 10)
Three-needle bind-off (page 24)

Size

7×5″ (18×12.5cm)

⊛ ⊛ ⊛

Gauge

32 stitches/16 rows=4″ (10cm)
in garter stitch

⊛ ⊛ ⊛

What You'll Need

Yarn: 330 yards (330m)
nylon eyelash yarn
We used: Plymouth Eros:
#4796 multicolor blues
and greens, 2 balls

Needles: US size 2 (2.75mm) double-pointed, set of 5; US size 2 (2.75mm) circular 16″ (40.5cm) long, 2 pairs

Notions: 2 separate lengths dark color, smooth worsted weight yarn for center of I-cord strap (60″ [152.5cm] longer for purse strap and 20″ [51cm] for purse trim); coilless pin; tapestry needle; sewing needle and thread to match; 1″ (2.5cm) glass bead or button (for embellishment only)

Note: Use knit into front and back of stitch (k1f&b) method for all increases.

Make the purse flap

Using double-pointed needles and long tail cast-on method, cast on 7 stitches.

Row 1: Knit 1, increase 1, knit 5, increase 1, knit 1. (9 stitches)

Rows 2–21: Knit across stitches, increasing 1 stitch at beginning and end of each row. (49 stitches)

Rows 22–23: Knit.

Row 24: Knit 1, increase 1, knit to end of row. (50 stitches)

Continue to knit back and forth in garter stitch without increasing until piece measures 1¾″ (4.5cm) from cast-on edge. Slide purse flap stitches onto circular needle, and hold until later. Cut yarn, leaving 4″ (10cm) tail.

Make I-cord strap

With working yarn and empty double-pointed needle, cast on 5 stitches. Work 5-stitch I-cord around dark-color worsted weight core yarn as follows: Slide 5 cast-on stitches to opposite end of needle (working yarn will be at far end of stitches). Place 1″–2″ (2.5cm–5cm) of 60″ (152.5cm) strand of core yarn over top of left needle, allowing this short tail to dangle temporarily on front side of work. Bring working yarn across back of stitches (passing *over* core yarn) to front of needle. Knit next row, flipping tail end over needle to back of work. *Slide stitches to opposite end of needle, passing working yarn *under* core yarn and to the front. Knit next row**. Repeat from * to **, trapping core yarn every time stitches are slipped to opposite end of needle. When strap measures 42″ (106.5cm) or desired length, leave cord on needle and follow directions to make purse.

Make the purse

On same needle as the 5 I-cord strap stitches, cast on 50 stitches for front section of purse. Then pick up 5 stitches from cast-on end of I-cord (60 stitches). The 5 I-cord stitches on each side of front stitches will become the 2 sides of the purse. Slip the 60 stitches of the flap onto second circular needle, leaving yarn attached to last stitch worked.

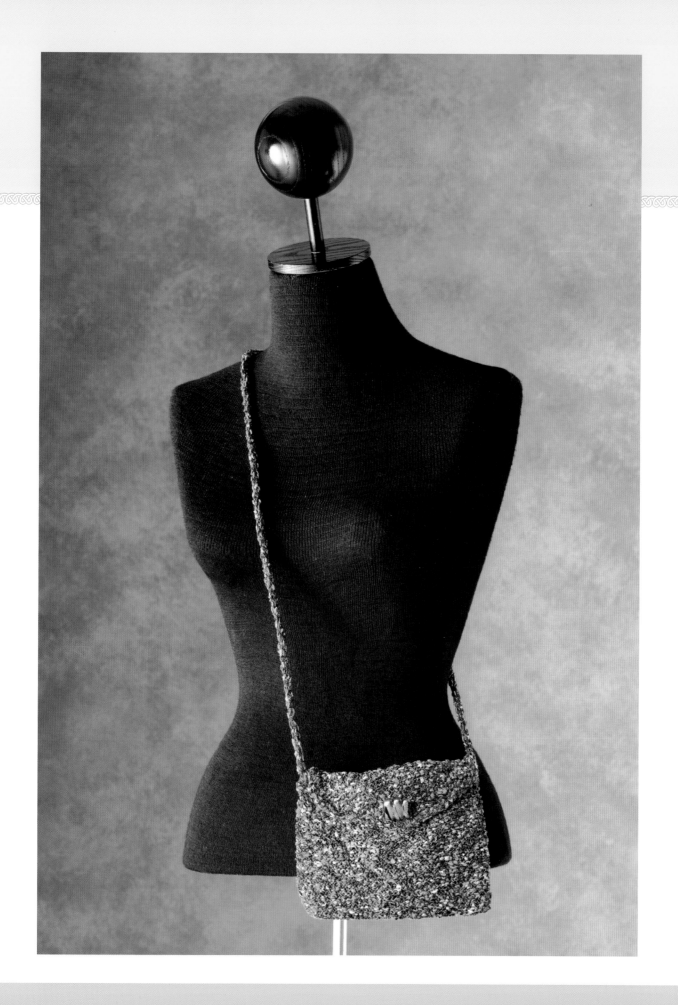

From this point, purse is worked circular, in rounds. To maintain garter stitch in circular knitting, alternate purl round with knit round. Join the 50 flap stitches (held on first circular needle) onto end of 60 stitches (110 stitches) to make pouch as follows:

Round 1: Using yarn still attached to end of circular needle with I-cords (now side stitches) and empty double-pointed needle, purl across 25 flap stitches. With a second empty needle, purl remaining 25 flap stitches. With a third empty needle, purl 5 side stitches and 25 front stitches. With a fourth empty needle, purl remaining 25 front stitches and 5 side stitches. Place a coilless pin in last stitch to mark end of round. The next stitch will be the beginning of each new round. Divide the 110 stitches onto 4 needles (27–28–27–28).

Round 2: Knit.

Round 3: Purl.

Round 4: Knit.

Repeat rounds 3 and 4 until purse measures 5″ (12.5cm) deep from beginning of circular knitting. End with purl row.

Finishing

Note: Seam is made on right side of work and forms a decorative, lightly ridged edge across the bottom.

Purse bottom: Transfer front, then back stitches onto separate circular needles. Make sure each needle has the same number of stitches (55). With wrong sides together, bind off front and back stitches using 3-needle bind-off.

With tapestry needle, weave in yarn tails to wrong side of work, leaving about 1″ (2.5cm) unwoven. Tack down woven-in part of yarn tails with sewing thread to secure. Trim free ends with scissors. With sewing thread and needle, use overhand stitch to reinforce areas where I-cords attach to sides of purse. Turn purse right-side out.

I-cord trim: With double-pointed needles, working yarn, and 20″ (51cm) strand of core yarn, cast on 3 stitches and knit I-cord around core yarn (in the same way the strap was done) for 20″ (51cm). Work last row as slip 1, knit 2 together, pass slipped stitch over. Cut yarn, and thread through last stitch to secure.

Using sewing needle and thread, and starting where one of the straps attaches to the body of the purse, carefully sew I-cord trim to outer edge of flap and along top edge on front of purse, finishing at the place where you started. Neatly stitch ends together. Secure all loose ends to wrong sides of work.

Sew decorative bead or button onto front of flap (button does not close purse flap).

Add a Little Razzle-Dazzle

There's a whole world of brilliant beads, glittering charms, and exciting ribbons and appliqués that add pizzazz to your knits. Visit any craft store, and be inspired by all the possibilities.

Sewing beads onto a simply knit sweater can turn it into a stunning piece of evening wear. And just look at the previous page to see how great a little knit handbag looks with a beautiful bead! Show a friend how well you know her by choosing inexpensive charms that reflect her interests, and use them to dress up a pillow or sachet. Surprise a new mom by adding appliqués to spell out the baby's name on a quick-knit afghan. (Just be sure to sew the appliqués securely in place so they don't become a choking hazard.)

When washing these items, place machine-washable items in a pillowcase and knot the top to keep charms and beads from being scratched in the washing machine.

Kids and Babies

From a hand-knit baby blanket to a one-of-a-kind layette, soft yarns and simple designs make a perfect present for a baby or child. Greet a new friend or family member with a personal gift made from the heart.

Color-Block Baby Blanket

To make this colorful baby blanket, knit thirty 6×6-inch squares and then sew them together. It's that easy! Each square is worked diagonally from corner to corner, with a color change in the center so each square looks like 2 triangles. It's a perfect project for on-the-go-knitting.

Designer: Berroco, Inc.

Techniques
Binding off—BO (page 14)
Casting on—CO (page 9)
Garter stitch (page 15)
Knit 1 into front and back loops—k1f&b (page 18)
Knit 2 together—k2tog (page 19)
Single crochet—sc (page 26)

Size
30×36" (76×91.5cm)

Gauge
12 stitches/24 rows=4" (10cm)
in garter stitch

What You'll Need
Yarn: Soft, bulky synthetic yarn, 270 yards (247m) in main color and about 180 yards (165m) in 4 other colors
We used: Berroco Plush (100% nylon): #1920 orange flash (color A), 2 balls; #1921 acid green (color B), 2 balls; #1922 pasty purple (color C), 2 balls; #1923 shocking pink (color D), 2 balls; #1924 jazzy turquoise (color E), 3 balls

Needles: US size 10 (6 mm)

Notions: Tapestry needle; size J/10 (6mm) crochet hook

Make the blanket

Square (make 6): With color A, cast on 1 stitch.

Next row: Increase 1 stitch using the knit into front and back loop method. (2 stitches)

Working in garter stitch, increase 1 stitch at the beginning of next 23 rows (25 stitches). Change to color D; knit 1 row. Decrease 1 stitch, using the knit 2 together method, at the beginning of each of next 24 rows (1 stitch). Cut yarn, leaving about 4" (10cm) tail; pull through remaining stitch to secure.

Working in the same manner, make a total of 6 squares using colors A and D; 8 squares using colors B and E; 6 squares using colors A and C; 4 squares using colors B and D; 4 squares using colors C and E; and 2 squares using colors C and D.

Finishing

When all squares are completed, sew them together using small, overhand sewing stitches, following the placement chart on page 74.

Edging: With crochet hook, join color E at any corner and work 1 row of single crochet around entire blanket, working 3 single crochet stitches in each corner. Join end of edging to beginning with a crochet slip stitch, working as follows: Insert hook under both top strands of first single crochet stitch, yarn over hook. In one motion, pull loop under both strands as well as the loop on the hook. Cut yarn, leaving about 4" (10cm) tail, and thread through loop on hook. Pull tight to secure stitch. Weave in all yarn tails to wrong side of work and through several stitches to secure.

 Tip

Where Am I?
You'll never again lose your place in your pattern when the phone rings or unexpected company knocks at the door. Just keep a pad of sticky notes in your bag, and stick one in place before leaving your knitting. Your place will be clearly marked when you pick your work up again.

Placement Chart for Squares

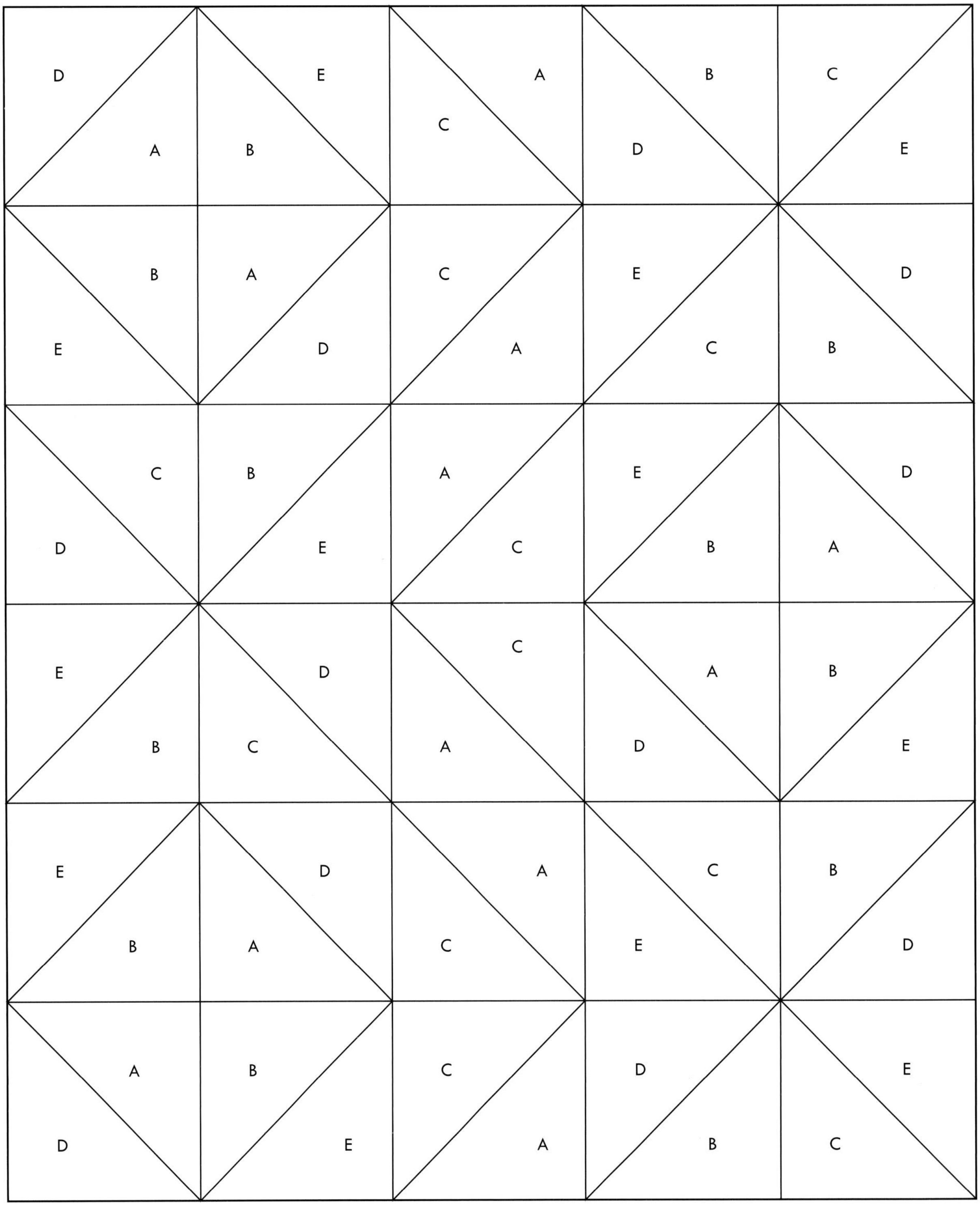

D   E   A   B   C

A   B   C   D   E

B   A   C   E   D

E   D   A   C   B

C   B   A   E   D

D   E   C   B   A

E   D   C   A   B

B   C   A   D   E

E   D   A   C   B

B   A   C   E   D

A   B   C   D   E

D   E   A   B   C

Baby's Best Booties

These snuggly booties are knitted in one piece—so they're as easy to make as they are adorable! They make a great gift for a new baby, and they're a terrific first project for a beginning knitter.

Designer: Lucie Sinkler

Techniques

Binding off—BO (page 14)
Casting on—CO (page 9)
Knit 2 stitches together—k2tog
(page 19)
Mattress stitch (page 23)
Simple cast-on (page 11)
Weaving in yarn tails (page 25)

Size

About 3 to 6 months, or best fit.
Finished foot length: 4½″ (11.5cm)

❀   ❀   ❀

Gauge

24 stitches/48 rows=4″ (10cm)
in garter stitch

❀   ❀   ❀

What You'll Need

Yarn: 100 yards medium-weight wool
yarn (about 110 yards/50g)
We used: Jo Sharp Handknitting Yarn
(100% wool) #309 cherry, 1 ball

Needles: US size 5 (3.75mm)

Notions: Tapestry needle; 1 yard (1m)
ribbon to match (for ties)

Note: Use simple cast-on method to make increases.

Make the booties

Cast on 46 stitches.

Rows 1 and 2: Knit.

Row 3: Knit 22, increase 1, knit 2, increase 1, knit 22. (48 stitches)

Row 4: Knit.

Row 5: Knit 22, increase 1, knit 4, increase 1, knit 22. (50 stitches)

Row 6: Knit.

Row 7: Knit 22, increase 1, knit 6, increase 1, knit 22. (52 stitches)

Row 8: Knit.

Row 9: Knit 22, increase 1, knit 8, increase 1, knit 22. (54 stitches)

Rows 10–12: Knit.

Row 13: Knit 22, increase 1, knit 10, increase 1, knit 22. (56 stitches)

Rows 14–16: Knit.

Row 17: Knit 22, increase 1, knit 12, increase 1, knit 22. (58 stitches)

Rows 18–30: Knit.

Row 31: Knit 14, increase 1, knit 10, increase 1, knit 10, increase 1, knit 10, increase 1, knit 14. (62 stitches)

Row 32: Knit.

Row 33: Bind off 13 stitches, knit to end of row. (49 stitches)

Row 34: Bind off 13 stitches, knit to end of row. (36 stitches)

Rows 35–46: Knit.

Row 47: Knit 2, knit 2 together, [knit 4, knit 2 together] 5 times, knit 2. (30 stitches)

Row 48: Knit.

Row 49: Knit 1, knit 2 together, [knit 3, knit 2 together] 5 times, knit 2. (24 stitches)

Row 50: Knit.

Row 51: Knit 1, knit 2 together, [knit 2, knit 2 together] 5 times, knit 1. (18 stitches)

Row 52: Knit.

Row 53: Knit 2 together to end of row. (9 stitches)

Finishing

Cut yarn about 18″ (46cm) from end of work. Thread yarn tail on tapestry needle and insert through remaining 9 stitches. Pull yarn firmly, closing toe stitches together. With same yarn and needle, seam instep edges together from toe to beginning of bind-off. *Don't seam bind-off edges.*

Insert needle and thread to wrong side of work, and weave through several stitches to secure. Cut another 18″ (46cm) of yarn from main ball; thread on tapestry needle. Fold bootie in half, and with right sides facing, sew back seam together using mattress stitch. Thread all yarn ends to wrong side of work, and weave through several stitches to secure.

Repeat all steps for second bootie.

Ties: Cut 1 yard (39.5cm) ribbon into 2 equal lengths. Thread 1 piece on tapestry needle; weave through stitches around ankle of bootie. Tie ends into a bow in front. Repeat for second bootie.

The Knitty-Gritty

From the Heart

Consider donating your time and talent by knitting for charity. There is so much need and so many ways you can help.

Our grandmothers called their work "Victory Knitting" as they supplied desperately needed socks, scarves, and warm hats for the troops in World War II. The men and women serving our country today still appreciate the gesture a hand-knit offers; it's a reminder they are respected, supported, and cared about.

Other charitable ideas: knit caps and hats for cancer patients; knit a quick, fashionable scarf out of eyelash yarn to be sold in a boutique, with profits going to support breast cancer research; knit tiny clothing for preemies, blankets for children in hospitals, and afghans and warm garments for homeless shelters.

Baby Kimono and Hat

This plush yarn really is as soft as it looks. Babies love the feel of it next to their skin, and you'll love the simple patterns and large needles that allow you to knit this layette in practically no time at all.

Designer: Berroco, Inc.

Size

Sweater

0–3 months: Chest (jacket closed)—19″ (48.5cm); length, 9″ (23cm)

3–6 months: Chest (jacket closed)—21″ (53.5cm); length, 10″ (25.5cm)

6–9 months: Chest (jacket closed), 23″ (58.5cm); length, 11″ (28cm)

Hat

Small: 15″ (38cm) around, 7″ (18cm) tall
Medium: 16″ (40.5cm) around, 7½″ (19cm) tall

❈ ❈ ❈

Gauge

12 stitches/20 rows=4″ (10cm)

❈ ❈ ❈

What You'll Need

Yarn: Soft synthetic bulky weight yarn: 180 [180, 270] yards (165m [165m, 247m]) for sweater; 90 yards (83m) for hat
We used: Berroco Plush (100% nylon): #1932 precious pink, 2 [2, 3] balls (sweater), 1 ball (hat)

Needles: US size 10 (6mm); US size 10 (6mm) set of 4 double-pointed; two size 5 (3.75 mm) double-pointed for I-cord

Notions: 4 stitch markers or small safety pins; tapestry needle; sewing needle and thread to match; 1¼ yards (1.15m) ribbon, ¼″ (6mm) wide

Note: Instructions are given for smallest size; all other sizes are listed in brackets. When only 1 number is given, it applies to all sizes.

Make the sweater

Make the back: Cast on 29 [32, 35] stitches. Work in stockinette stitch until piece measures 5″ [5½″, 6″] (12.5cm [14cm, 15cm]) in length from cast-on edge, ending with wrong-side row. With stitch markers or safety pins, mark beginning and end of last row to indicate beginning of armholes. Leave markers in place until finishing. Work even until armhole measures 4″ [4½″, 5″] (10cm [11.5cm, 12.5cm]) from markers, ending with wrong-side row. Bind off all stitches.

Make the left front: Cast on 23 [26, 29] stitches. Work in stockinette stitch until piece measures 5″ [5½″, 6″] (12.5cm [14cm, 15cm]) from beginning, ending with right-side row. With stitch marker or safety pin, mark beginning of last row to indicate beginning of armhole. Leave marker in place until finishing.

Shape the neck

Row 1: (wrong side) Bind off 3 [4, 5] stitches, purl to end of row. (20 [22, 24] stitches)

Row 2: (right side) Knit.

Row 3: Bind off 3 stitches, purl to end of row. (17 [19, 21] stitches)

Row 4: Knit.

Row 5: Bind off 2 stitches, purl to end of row. (15 [17, 19] stitches)

Rows 6 and 7: Repeat rows 4 and 5. (13 [15, 17] stitches)

Row 8: Knit to last 3 stitches (neck edge), knit 2 together, knit 1. (12 [14, 16] stitches)

Row 9: Purl.

Repeat rows 8 and 9 three [4, 5] more times (9 [10, 11] stitches). Work even in stockinette stitch until armhole measures 4″ [4½″, 5″] (10cm [11.5cm, 12.5cm]) from marker, ending with wrong-side row.

Techniques

Backstitch (page 23)
Binding off–BO (page 14)
Casting on–CO (page 9)
Circular stockinette stitch (page 15)
Double-pointed needles (page 16)
Increases (page 17)
Knit 2 together–k2tog (page 19)
Mattress stitch (page 23)
Purl 2 together–p2tog (page 19)
Stockinette stitch–St st (page 15)

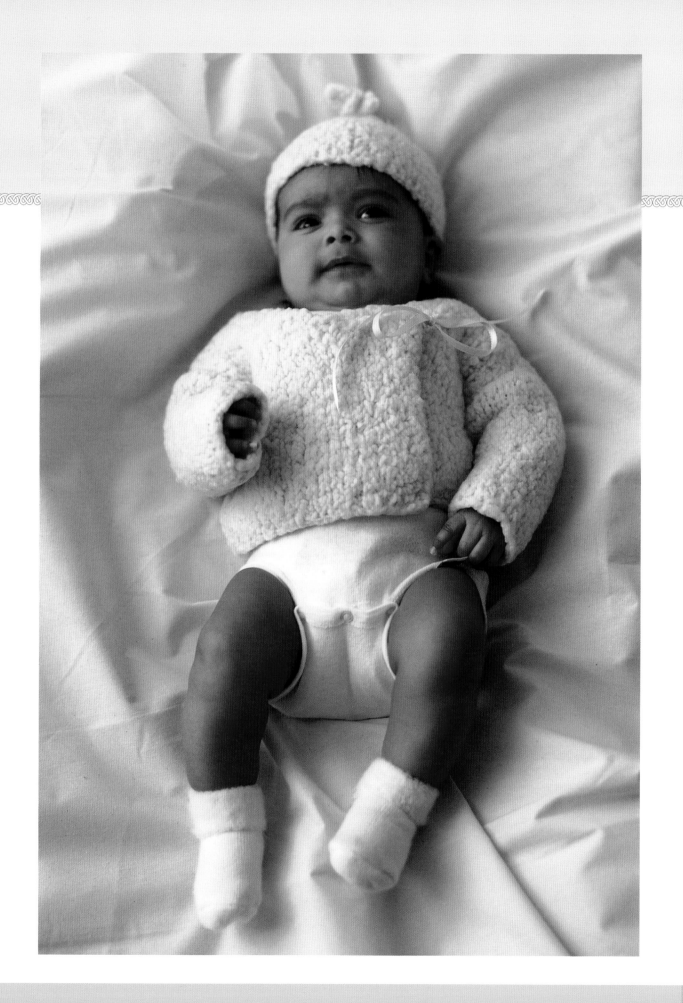

Next row: Bind off all stitches. Cut yarn, leaving 6″ (15cm) tail. Thread tapestry needle and weave tail through a few stitches on wrong side of work to secure. Trim end, leaving about ¼″ (6mm).

Make the right front: Work same as left front until piece measures 5″ [5½″, 6″] (12.5cm [14cm, 15cm]) from beginning, ending with wrong-side row. Reverse all shaping as follows:

Shape the neck

Row 1: (right side) Bind off 3 [4, 5] stitches, knit to end of row. (20 [22, 24] stitches)

Row 2: (wrong side) Purl.

Row 3: Bind off 3 stitches, knit to end of row. (17 [19, 21] stitches)

Row 4: Purl.

Row 5: Bind off 2 stitches, knit to end of row. (15 [17, 19] stitches)

Rows 6 and 7: Repeat rows 4 and 5. (13 [15, 17] stitches)

Row 8: Purl to last 3 stitches (neck edge); purl 2 together, purl 1. (12 [14, 16] stitches)

Row 9: Knit.

Repeat rows 8 and 9 three [4, 5] more times. [9 (10, 11) stitches]

Work even in stockinette stitch until armhole measures 4″ [4½″, 5″] (10cm [11.5cm, 12.5cm]) from marker, ending with wrong-side row.

Next row: Bind off all stitches. Cut yarn, leaving 6″ (15cm) tail. Thread tapestry needle and weave tail through a few stitches on wrong side of work to secure.

Make the sleeves: Cast on 18 [19, 20] stitches. Work even in stockinette stitch for 1″ (2.5cm), ending with wrong-side row.

Increase row: (right side) Knit 1, knit into front and back of next stitch, knit to last 2 stitches, knit into front and back of next stitch, knit 1. (20 [21, 22] stitches)

Work remaining sleeve increases as follows:

0–3 month size: Work increase row every 10th row 2 times. (24 stitches)

3–6 month size: Work increase row every 8th row 3 times. (27 stitches)

6–9 month size: Work increase row every 6th row once, then every 8th row 3 times. (30 stitches)

All sizes: Work even in stockinette stitch until sleeve measures 6″ [7″, 8″] (15cm [18cm, 20.5cm]) from cast-on edge, ending with wrong-side row.

Next row: (right side) Bind off all stitches.

Repeat all steps for second sleeve.

Finishing

Sew shoulder seams together with backstitch seam. With right sides together, pin sleeves to armholes, working between armhole markers. Sew sleeves to armholes using backstitch. Remove pins and markers. With right sides facing out, use mattress stitch to seam side edges together and sleeve edges together.

Attaching ribbons: Cut ribbon into 4 equal pieces, and turn under raw edges. With sewing needle and thread, whipstitch end of first ribbon piece to right front edge at beginning of neck shaping. Sew end of second ribbon piece to left front edge at beginning of neck shaping. Lap right front over left front, and mark left front at the place where right front edge ends. Open jacket, and place marker on the wrong side of right front at the place where the left front edge ends when the jacket is closed. Whipstitch remaining 2 ribbons in place. Remove pins and markers. Weave in all loose ends to wrong sides, and secure.

Make the hat

With larger size double-pointed needles, cast on 45 [48] stitches. Divide stitches evenly between 3 needles; 15 [16] stitches on each. Join stitches into a circle, taking care not to twist the stitches. Place a marker at first stitch to indicate beginning of round. (You may prefer to attach a safety pin to the first stitch as your marker and move upward with each new round.) Work in circular stockinette stitch for 2″ (5cm).

Next round: (decreases) *Knit 5 [6] stitches, knit 2 together, knit 6, knit 2 together**; repeat from * to ** to end of round. (39 [42] stitches)

Next 3 rounds: Knit.

Next round: (decreases) *Knit 4 [5] stitches, knit 2 together, knit 5, knit 2 together**; repeat from * to ** to end of round. (33 [36] stitches)

Next 3 rounds: Knit.

Next round: (decreases) *Knit 3 [4] stitches, knit 2 together, knit 4, knit 2 together**; repeat from * to ** to end of round. (27 [30] stitches)

Next 3 rounds: Knit.

Next round: (decreases) *Knit 2 [3] stitches, knit 2 together, knit 3, knit 2 together**; repeat from * to ** to end of round. (21 stitches [24] stitches)

Next 3 rounds: Knit.

Next round: (decreases) *Knit 1 [2] stitches, knit 2 together, knit 2, knit 2 together**; repeat from * to ** to end of round. (15 [18] stitches)

Next 3 rounds: Knit.

Next round: (decreases) *Knit 2 together, knit 1**; repeat from * to ** to end of round. (10 [12] stitches)

Medium size only:

Next 3 rounds: Knit.

Next round: *Knit 2 together**; repeat from * to ** to end of round. (6 stitches)

Both sizes:

Next round: *Knit 2 together**; repeat from * to ** to end of round. (5 [3] stitches)

Small size only:

Next round: Knit 1, *knit 2 together**; repeat from * to ** to end of round. (3 stitches)

Both sizes: Remove stitch marker, and slip remaining 3 stitches onto smaller size double-pointed needle.

Make I-cord: *Knit 3, do not turn work. Slide stitches to opposite end of needle, bringing working yarn from back of work to front; repeat from * until I-cord measures 5″ (12.5cm). Cut yarn, leaving 10″ (25.5cm) tail. Thread tail on tapestry needle, and draw through 3 stitches. Gently pull yarn to gather stitches and close I-cord. Weave yarn tail into center of I-cord to secure. Tie overhand knot, forming loop in I-cord (see photo).

Size Chart

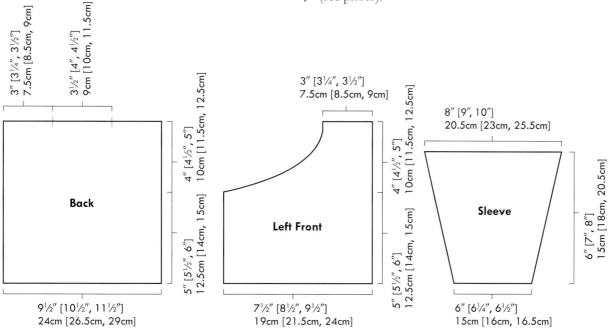

Back — 3″ [3¼″, 3½″] 7.5cm [8.5cm, 9cm]; 3½″ [4″, 4½″] 9cm [10cm, 11.5cm]; 4″ [4½″, 5″] 10cm [11.5cm, 12.5cm]; 5″ [5½″, 6″] 12.5cm [14cm, 15cm]; 9½″ [10½″, 11½″] 24cm [26.5cm, 29cm]

Left Front — 3″ [3¼″, 3½″] 7.5cm [8.5cm, 9cm]; 4″ [4½″, 5″] 10cm [11.5cm, 12.5cm]; 5″ [5½″, 6″] 12.5cm [14cm, 15cm]; 7½″ [8½″, 9½″] 19cm [21.5cm, 24cm]

Sleeve — 8″ [9″, 10″] 20.5cm [23cm, 25.5cm]; 6″ [7″, 8″] 15cm [18cm, 20.5cm]; 6″ [6¼″, 6½″] 15cm [16cm, 16.5cm]

Barnyard Finger Puppets

Handmade toys are a rarity these days. For an adorable gift that's destined to become a cherished favorite, why not knit a set of darling finger puppets? Parents will *ooh* and *aah* over your thoughtfulness, and children will love the toys!

Designer: Lucie Sinkler

Techniques

Binding off—BO (page 14)
Casting on—CO (page 9)
Crochet chain (page 26)
Duplicate stitch (page 25)
I-cord (page 21)
Joining yarns (page 21)
Knit 2 together—k2tog (page 19)
Make 1 increase—m1 (page 18)
Purl 2 together—p2tog (page 19)
Slip slip knit decrease—ssk (page 19)
Slip stitch (page 17)
Stockinette stitch—St st (page 15)
Working with 2 colors (page 20)

Size

2½" to 3" (6.5cm to 7.5cm) each

⊗　⊗　⊗

Gauge

22 stitches/36 rows=4" (10cm)
in stockinette stitch

⊗　⊗　⊗

What You'll Need

Yarn: Worsted weight wool: 15 yards (14m) main color for each puppet; 5 yards contrasting colors as needed; scrap yarn
We used: Cascade Yarns Cascade 220 (100% wool) 5–15 yards (5–9m) each white, brown, red, black, orange, navy; Dale of Norway Dale Baby Ull (100% wool) used doubled, 15 yards (14m) each yellow, pink, beige

Needles: US size 3 (3.25mm) straight; 2 US size 3 (3.25mm) double-pointed

Notions: Tapestry needle; US size D/3 (3.25mm) crochet hook

Note: If using yarns other than worsted weight, such as Baby Ull, work with 2 strands held together as 1 throughout. If working with worsted weight yarn, use single strand.

Make the duck

Using yellow yarn, cast on 15 stitches. Work 12 rows of stockinette stitch.

Make the bill

Row 1: (right side) With yellow yarn, knit 5 stitches. Drop yellow yarn and join orange yarn; knit 5 stitches. Leave remaining stitches on needle; turn work.

Work short rows for shaping as follows:

Row 2: Slip 1 stitch, purl 3, leave remaining stitches on needle, turn work.

Row 3: Slip 1, knit 2, leave remaining stitches on needle, turn work.

Row 4: Slip 1, purl 1, leave remaining stitches on needle, turn work.

Row 5: Slip 1, knit 1, leave remaining stitches on needle, turn work.

Row 6: Slip 1, purl 2, leave remaining stitches on needle, turn work.

Row 7: Slip 1, knit 3, leave remaining stitches on needle, turn work.

Row 8: Slip 1, purl 4. Drop orange yarn and pick up yellow; purl across row.

Work 5 more rows of stockinette stitch.

Shape top of head

Row 1: (right side) Knit 1, [knit 2 together] 7 times. (8 stitches)
Row 2: Purl.
Row 3: [Knit 2 together] 4 times. (4 stitches)

Cut yarn, leaving 6" (15cm) tail. Thread yarn tail on tapestry needle, and pull through 4 remaining stitches to close top.

Make the eyes: With small amount black yarn threaded on tapestry needle, work 2 duplicate stitches above beak for eyes.

Finishing

Using yellow yarn tail at top of head, fold puppet in half, thread tapestry needle, and close back seam with mattress stitch. Weave in loose ends to wrong side of work, and secure.

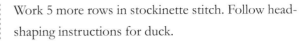

Make the pig

Using pink yarn, cast on 15 stitches. Work 12 rows of stockinette stitch, ending with wrong-side row.

Form the snout
Row 1: (right side) Knit 10 stitches, turn work.
Row 2: Slip 1 stitch, purl 3, turn.
Row 3: Slip 1, knit 3, turn.
Row 4: Slip 1, purl 3, turn.
Row 5: Slip 1, knit to end of row.
Work 5 more rows in stockinette stitch.

Shape top of head: Follow head-shaping instructions for duck (page 82).

Form the ears: Using pink yarn, cast on 5 stitches.
Row 1: Slip slip knit decrease; knit 1; knit 2 together. (3 stitches)
Row 2: Purl 3 together. Cut yarn, and pull through remaining stitch.
Repeat for second ear.

Make the eyes and nose: With black yarn threaded on tapestry needle, embroider 2 straight lines, each about stitch length, for nostrils. Work 2 duplicate stitches above nose for eyes.

Finishing

Thread tapestry needle with pink yarn tail remaining from head shaping, fold puppet in half, and close back seam using mattress stitch. Sew ears in position. Weave all loose ends to wrong side, and secure.

Make the horse

With brown yarn, cast on 15 stitches. Work 12 rows in stockinette stitch.

Form the nose: Beginning on right side of work, knit 10, [turn work, slip 1, purl 4, turn, slip 1, knit 4] 3 times. Knit 5.

Work 5 more rows in stockinette stitch. Follow head-shaping instructions for duck.

Make the ears and eyes: Using double strand of brown yarn and crochet hook, make a slipknot. Make 2 additional chain stitches, pulling yarn tail through last loop. Thread end on tapestry needle; sew ear in place. Repeat to make second ear. With 10″ (25.5cm) black yarn threaded on tapestry needle, embroider 2 straight lines for nostrils, and work 2 duplicate stitches for eyes.

Finishing

Fold puppet in half, and close back seam using mattress stitch.

Add the mane: Cut 7 strands black yarn, each about 4″ (10cm) long. Fold 1 strand in half and thread tapestry needle. Insert needle and yarn through 1 stitch on top of horse's head and between ears. Pull both loose ends of strand together and insert them through folded yarn end; pull ends to tighten knot. Work remaining 6 strands the same, 1 at a time, inserting each folded strand into back seam about 1 stitch down from previous strand and knotting as above. Weave all loose ends to wrong side, and secure.

Make the farmer

With blue yarn, cast on 15 stitches. Work 7 rows in stockinette stitch, ending with right-side row.
Row 8: (wrong side) Purl 6 stitches with red yarn, purl 3 with blue, purl 6 with red.
Row 9: Knit 6 stitches with red, knit 3 with blue, knit 6 with red.
Row 10: Repeat row 8.
Row 11: With red yarn, knit 4 stitches; slip slip knit decrease; knit 3; knit 2 together; knit 4. (13 stitches)
Row 12: Purl row with red yarn.
Row 13: With red yarn, knit 4 stitches; slip slip knit decrease; knit 1; knit 2 together; knit 4 (11 stitches). Cut yarn.

Make the head

Row 14: Continuing work on same stitches, join beige yarn and purl row.

Row 15: With beige, [knit 2, make 1] 5 times, knit 1. (16 stitches)

Rows 16–22: Beginning with purl row (wrong side), work in stockinette stitch. End with purl row.

Row 23: [Knit 2 together] 8 times. (8 stitches)

Row 24: Purl.

Row 25: [Knit 2 together] 4 times. (4 stitches)
Cut yarn, leaving 4″ (10cm) tail. Thread yarn tail on tapestry needle and pull through remaining 4 stitches to close top of head. Thread tail to wrong side, and secure.

Make the arms: With red yarn and double-pointed needle, cast on 3 stitches. Work I-cord for 5 rows, change to beige, and work 3 more rows of I-cord. Cut yarn; thread tail through tapestry needle and pull through remaining I-cord stitches to close end. Secure all I-cord ends inside arm. Repeat to make second arm.

Make the ears: Thread tapestry needle with 4″ (10cm) beige yarn. Insert through bottom of 1 stitch about halfway up side of head, then insert needle through upper part of same stitch to make loop for ear. Repeat on opposite side of head for second ear. Weave yarn tails to wrong side, and secure.

Form mouth and eyes: With black yarn threaded on tapestry needle, make 2 eyes using duplicate stitch. Use red yarn to embroider 3 stitches in a slight curve for mouth.

Finishing

Weave all ends to wrong side, and secure. Fold puppet in half, and close back seam with mattress stitch. Sew arms in position.

Add hair: With black yarn threaded on tapestry needle, make several long stitches over center top of head (see photo). Weave in remaining loose ends to wrong side.

Make the cow

Using white yarn, cast on 15 stitches. Work 4 rows in stockinette stitch.

Row 5: Knit 4 stitches with white, knit 3 with black, knit 8 with white.

Row 6: Purl 7 stitches with white, purl 5 with black, purl 3 with white.

Row 7: Knit 3 stitches with white, knit 5 with black, knit 7 with white.

Row 8: Purl 7 stitches with white, purl 4 with black, purl 4 with white.

Row 9: Knit 5 stitches with white, knit 2 with black, knit 8 with white.

Row 10: Purl 4 stitches with white, purl 2 with black, purl 3 with white, purl 1 with black, purl 5 with white.

Row 11: Knit 8 stitches with white, knit 4 with black, knit 3 with white.

Row 12: Purl 4 stitches with white, purl 2 with black, purl 9 with white.

Row 13: Continue in white only: Knit 10, [turn work, slip 1, purl 4, turn work, slip 1, knit 4] 3 times. Knit 5.

Row 14: Purl.

Row 15: Knit.

Row 16: Purl.

Row 17: Knit 6, [turn work, slip 1, purl 1, turn work, slip 1, knit 1] 3 times, knit 5, [turn work, slip 1, purl 1, turn work, slip 1, knit 1] 3 times, knit 4.

Row 18: Purl.

Follow head-shaping instructions for duck (page 82).

Make nostrils, eyes, and ears: With 12″ (30.5cm) black yarn threaded on tapestry needle, embroider 2 straight lines, each about stitch length, for nostrils. Work duplicate stitches for 2 eyes, and make 2 French knots for horns on top of head (see photo).

Finishing

Weave in all loose ends to wrong side. Thread tapestry needle with yarn tail from top, and close back seam with mattress stitch.

Honeycomb Stroller Blanket

Unlike most typical baby blankets, this one features a unique honeycomb pattern. It may look complicated, but the pattern is actually easy enough to master. The blanket's small size, perfect for a stroller or crib, is another welcome feature.

Designer: Terry Kimbrough

Techniques
Binding off—BO (page 14)
Casting on—CO (page 9)
Picking up stitches (page 22)
Ribbing (page 15)
Slip stitch purlwise (page 17)

Size
Approximately 24×32″ (61×81.5cm)

⊛　⊛　⊛

Gauge
19 stitches and 24 rows=4″ (10cm)
in pattern

⊛　⊛　⊛

What You'll Need
Yarn: Sport weight yarn: about 6oz (170g) each in 3 colors
We used: Bernat Baby Coordinates (75.2% acrylic, 22.2% acetate): Lavender (main color); mint green (color A); peach (color B), 1 ball each

Needles: US size 10 (6mm)

Notion: Tapestry needle

Note: Carry unused yarn loosely along edge; do not cut yarn at end of each color.

Make the blanket

With color B, cast on 100 stitches very loosely.

Rows 1 and 2: Knit.

Row 3: (right side) With color A, knit 1, with yarn in back slip 2 as if to purl, *knit 6, with yarn in back slip 2 as if to purl**; repeat from * to ** across to last stitch, knit 1.

Row 4: Purl 1, with yarn in front slip 2 as if to purl, *purl 6, with yarn in front slip 2 as if to purl**; repeat from * to ** across row to last stitch, purl 1.

Rows 5–8: Repeat rows 3 and 4 twice more.

Rows 9 and 10: Change to color B; knit.

Row 11: With main color, knit 5, with yarn in back slip 2 as if to purl, *knit 6, with yarn in back slip 2 as if to purl**. Repeat from * to ** across to last 5 stitches; knit 5.

Row 12: Purl 5, with yarn in front slip 2 as if to purl, *purl 6, with yarn in front slip 2 as if to purl**; repeat from * to ** across to last 5 stitches, purl 5.

Rows 13–16: Repeat rows 11 and 12 twice more.

Rows 17–218: Repeat rows 1–16 twelve times; then repeat rows 1–10 once more.

With color B, bind off all stitches very loosely.

Make the border:

Side edge Using main color, with right side facing pick up 108 stitches evenly spaced across side edge.

Rows 1–5: Work in knit 1, purl 1 ribbing across 108 stitches.
Bind off all stitches very loosely.

Repeat for other side edge.

Lower edge Using main color, with right side facing working across cast-on edge, pick up 86 stitches evenly spaced across lower edge.

Rows 1–5: Work in knit 1, purl 1 ribbing across 86 stitches.
Bind off all stitches very loosely.

Repeat for upper edge across bound-off edge.

Weave in all yarn ends to wrong side of work.

Hooded Jacket and Booties

Super-fast to make, and soft as a baby's bottom! Make several, and keep them on hand for baby showers. Bright, joyful colors mean that this modern layette works for both boys and girls.

Designer: Lucie Sinkler

Techniques

Binding off—BO (page 14)

Casting on—CO (page 9)

Knit 2 together—k2tog (page 19)

Make 1 increase—m1 (page 18)

Mattress stitch (page 23)

Purlwise (page 25)

Ribbing (page 15)

Slip 1, knit 2 together, pass slipped stitch over—sl 1, k2tog, psso (page 21)

Stockinette stitch—St st (page 15)

Weaving in yarn tails (page 25)

Size

Jacket

3–6 months: chest size—19″ (51cm)

6–12 months: chest size—21″ (54cm)

12–18 months: chest size—23″ (59cm)

Booties

3–6 months

⊗   ⊗   ⊗

Gauge

13 stitches/22 rows=4″ (10cm)

in stockinette stitch

⊗   ⊗   ⊗

What You'll Need

Yarn: Soft, synthetic bulky weight yarn, about 270 [360, 360] yards (247m [330m, 330m])

We used: Berroco Plush (100% nylon) #1951 crayon mix, 3 [4, 4] balls

Needles: US size 10 (6mm)

Notions: Tapestry needle; straight pins; 9″ [9½″, 10½″] (23cm [24cm, 26.5cm]) separating zipper; sewing needle and thread to match; stitch holder

---

Note: Instructions are given for smallest size; all other sizes are listed in brackets. When only 1 number is given, it applies to all sizes.

Make the jacket

Back

Cast on 33 [37, 41] stitches. Work 2 rows of knit 1, purl 1 ribbing. Change to stockinette stitch, and continue until piece measures 6¾″ [7″, 7½″] (17cm [18cm, 19cm]). End with purl row.

Armhole shaping

Next row: (right side) Bind off 3 stitches at beginning of row, then knit to end of row. (30 [34, 38] stitches)

Next row: (wrong side) Bind off first 3 stitches purlwise, purl to end of row. (27 [31, 35] stitches)

Continue in stockinette stitch until back measures 11″ [11½″, 12½″] (28cm [29cm, 31.5cm]). Bind off all stitches.

Left front

Cast on 17 [19, 21]stitches. Work 2 rows of knit 1, purl 1 ribbing. Change to stockinette stitch; continue until piece measures 6¾″ [7″, 7½″] (17cm [18cm, 19cm]), ending with purl row.

Armhole shaping

Next row: (right side) Bind off 3 stitches, knit to end of row. (14 [16, 18] stitches)

Continue in stockinette stitch for 2¼″ [2½″, 3″] (5.5cm [6.5cm, 7.5cm]), ending with a knit row.

Neck shaping

Next row: (wrong side) Bind off 3 stitches purlwise at beginning of row, then purl to end. (11 [13, 15] stitches)

Next row: (right side) Knit.

Next row: (wrong side) Bind off 2 stitches purlwise, purl to end of row. (9 [11, 13] stitches)

Next row: (right side) Knit.

Next row: (wrong side) Bind off 1 stitch, purl to end of row. (8 [10, 12] stitches)

Continue in stockinette stitch until front measures same as back—11″ [11½″, 12½″] (28cm [29cm, 31.5cm]). Bind off all stitches.

Right front

Make as left front, reversing shaping as follows. Cast on 17 [19, 21] stitches. Work 2 rows knit 1, purl 1 ribbing. Change to stockinette stitch for 6¾″ [7″, 7½″] (17cm [18cm, 19cm]). End with knit row.

Armhole shaping

Next row: (wrong side) Bind off 3 stitches, purl to end of row. (14 [16, 18] stitches)

Continue in stockinette stitch for 2¼″ [2½″, 3″] (5.5cm [6.5cm, 7.5cm]). End with purl row.

Neck shaping

Next row: (right side) Bind off 3 stitches, knit to end of row. (11 [13, 15] stitches)

Next row: (wrong side) Purl.

Next row: (right side) Bind off 2 stitches, knit to end of row. (9 [11, 13] stitches)

Next row: (wrong side) Purl.

Next row: Bind off 1 stitch, knit to end of row. (8 [10, 12] stitches)

Continue in stockinette stitch until front measures same as back—11″ [11½″, 12½″] (28cm [29cm, 31.5cm]). Bind off all stitches.

Sleeve

Cast on 20 stitches. Work 2 rows knit 1, purl 1 ribbing.

Sleeve shaping

Next row: Knit 1, make 1, knit 18, make 1, knit 1. (22 stitches)

Continue in stockinette stitch, increasing same way every sixth row until there are 32 [34, 36] stitches on needle. Work even in stockinette stitch without

further increases until sleeve measures 7″ [7½″, 8″] (18cm [19cm, 20.5cm]). End with purl row. Bind off.

Repeat all steps for second sleeve.

Hood

Cast on 5 stitches.

Row 1: Knit.

Row 2: Purl. At the end of the row, cast on 2 stitches using either cable cast-on or simple cast-on method.

Row 3: Knit. (7 stitches)

Row 4: Purl. Cast on 2 stitches.

Row 5: Knit. (9 stitches)

Row 6: Purl. Cast on 3 stitches.

Row 7: Knit. (12 stitches)

Row 8: Purl. Cast on 4 stitches.

Row 9: Knit. (16 stitches)

Rows 10–20 (even rows only): Purl.

Row 11: Knit 1, make 1, knit 15. (17 stitches)

Row 13: Knit 1, make 1, knit 16. (18 stitches)

Row 15: Knit 1, make 1, knit 17. (19 stitches)

Row 17: Knit 1, make 1, knit 18. (20 stitches)

Row 19: Knit 1, make 1, knit 19. (21 stitches)

Work even without further increases until hood measures 8½″ (21.5cm) from cast-on edge. End with right-side row. *Don't bind off.* Place marker to indicate end of first half.

Second side of hood: Work even for 5″ (12.5cm) from stitch marker. On next wrong-side row, begin with row 20 and work back to row 1. Mirror shaping by decreasing on rows where increases were made, and bind off stitches on the rows where stitches were cast on. When row 1 is finished, work should measure 8½″ (21.5cm) from stitch marker. Bind off remaining 5 stitches.

Finishing

Sew fronts to back piece at shoulders using mattress stitch with yarn threaded on tapestry needle. Fold hood in half, and sew seam from center neck to tip of hood. Pin hood to neck opening, matching front and hood edges. Sew hood in place from right side with mattress stitch. Pin sleeve tops to armholes, and stitch in place using backstitch. Sew side seams and sleeves with mattress stitch. Baste zipper in position, placing edges of knitted pieces next to teeth. With sewing thread, sew zipper in place using backstitch along the edge of knitted fronts. Whipstitch edges of zipper tape in place from wrong side. Remove all pins. Weave yarn ends on wrong side of jacket.

Make the booties

Cast on 16 stitches.

Row 1: (right side) Purl.

Row 2: (wrong side) Knit 1, *make 1, knit 1**; repeat from * to ** to end of row. (31 stitches)

Row 3: Purl.

Row 4: Knit.

Row 5: Purl.

Row 6: Knit 12, knit 2 together, knit 3, knit 2 together, knit 12. (29 stitches)

Row 7: Purl.

Row 8: Knit 11, knit 2 together, knit 3, knit 2 together, knit 11. (27 stitches)

Row 9: Purl.

Row 10: Knit 12, slip 1, knit 2 together, pass the slipped stitch over, knit 12. (25 stitches)

Row 11: Purl.

Row 12: Knit 9, bind off 7, knit to end of row (18 stitches). Place first set of 9 stitches on holder.

Row 13: Knit. (9 stitches)

Row 14: Purl.

Rows 15–23: Continue in reverse stockinette (purl on right side, knit on wrong side, repeat rows 13–14). Bind off on row 24. Cut yarn. Transfer stitches from holder back onto needle. With wrong side of bootie facing, rejoin yarn at the end of bind-off stitches. Repeat rows 13–24. Fold bootie piece in half. With threaded tapestry needle, sew instep together (the 7 bound-off stitches in the center). Sew cast-on edges (underfoot) together with whipstitch. With right side facing, sew back seam together with mattress stitch up to the reverse stockinette stitch, then turn bootie to wrong side to finish seam. Weave ends to wrong side, and secure. Turn bootie to right side, and fold cuff back.

Repeat all steps for second bootie.

Easy Does It

Is your yarn fuzzy, furry, or flimsy? Does it have more than one color in it? If it does, it's best to choose a pattern with simple stitches to let the complexity of the yarn shine through. In general, the simpler the yarn, the more complicated, lacy, or textured pattern you can use; the more complex the yarn, the simpler the pattern.

Stripes-and-Solids Sweater

A casual, comfortable toddler sweater that's this cute *and* easy to make—who could resist?
Knit it in these bold colors, or choose a mix of pastels to make the design even sweeter.

Designer: Phyllis Fishberg

Size

2 years: chest—27″ (68.5cm)
4 years: chest—28½″ (72.5cm)
6 years: chest—30″ (76cm)
8 years: chest—32″ (81.5cm)

❀ ❀ ❀

Gauge

20 stitches/26 rows=4″ (10cm) in
stockinette stitch on size 6 needles

❀ ❀ ❀

What You'll Need

Yarn: Acrylic and wool worsted weight
blend: 215 yards (197m) color A;
215 yards (197m) color B;
215 yards (197m) color C; 430 [430,
430, 645] yards (394m
[394m, 394m, 591m]) color D
We used: JCA/Reynolds Signature
(80% acrylic/20% wool): #57 navy
(color A), 1 skein; #81 gray (color B),
1 skein; #1 white (color C),
1 skein; #67 cranberry (color D),
2 [2, 2, 3] skeins

Needles: US size 6 (4mm); US size
5 (3.75mm) circular needles
16″ (40.5cm) in length

Notions: Stitch holder; tapestry needle

Note: Instructions are given for smallest
size; all other sizes are listed in brackets. When only 1 number is given, it
applies to all sizes.

Make the back

With size 6 needles and color A, cast
on 68 [72, 76, 80] stitches. Work
knit 1, purl 1 ribbing for 4 [6, 6, 8]
rows. Change to color B, and work
in stockinette stitch for 5″ [5½″, 6″,
6½″] (12.5cm [14cm, 15cm,
16.5cm]).

Begin armhole: Change to color A; working in stockinette stitch, bind
off 5 stitches at beginning of next 2 rows (58 [62, 66, 70] stitches).
Change to color C; work even for 6 [6, 6, 8] rows. Change to color A,
work even for 2 rows. Change to color D, and work even until armhole
measures 5½″ [6″, 6½″, 7″] (14cm [15cm, 16.5cm, 18cm]). Bind off all
stitches.

Make the front

Work same as back until piece measures 2½″ [3″, 3″, 4″] (6.5cm [7.5cm,
7.5cm, 10cm]) from armhole bind-off. On next right-side row, knit
21 [22, 24, 25] stitches. Place next 16 [18, 18, 20] stitches on holder. Join
another ball of color D, and finish knitting row. Work both sides of
neckline at same time: On next row (wrong side), purl to last 2 stitches
before neck edge, purl 2 together. Drop yarn, pick up next yarn on other
side of neck edge, purl 2 together, purl to end of row. Continue in stockinette stitch, decreasing at neck edge on wrong-side rows 2 [3, 3, 4] more
times (18 [18, 20, 20] stitches each side). Work even until front measures
same as back. Bind off both sets of stitches and join shoulders to back
shoulders using backstitch.

Make the neckband

With circular needles and color D, pick up and knit 22 [26, 26, 28]
stitches across back neck, 10 [11, 12, 13] stitches along first side of front

Techniques

Backstitch (page 23)
Binding off–BO (page 14)
Casting on–CO (page 9)
Joining new colors (page 21)
Mattress stitch (page 23)
Picking up stitches (page 22)
Purl 2 together–p2tog (page 19)
Ribbing (page 15)
Slip slip knit decrease–ssk (page 19)
Stockinette stitch–St st (page 15)
Working with circular needles
(page 16)

neck, 16 (18, 18, 20) stitches from holder, and 10 [11,12,13] stitches along second side of front neck (58 [66, 68, 74] stitches). Work knit 1, purl 1 ribbing for 4 [6, 6, 8] rows. Bind off loosely.

Make the sleeves

With color D, pick up and knit 50 [56, 60, 64] stitches between bound-off edges of armhole. Work in stockinette stitch for 1½″ (3.8cm), then begin decreasing 1 stitch on each side every 6th row 6 [7, 7, 8] times (38 [42, 46, 48] stitches). Work even until sleeve measures 8″ [8½″, 9″, 9½″] (20.5cm [21.5cm, 23cm, 24cm]) from armhole, or to desired length. Decrease 4 [6, 8, 10] stitches on next wrong-side row (34 [36, 38, 38] stitches). Change to color A, and knit 1 row. Change to knit 1, purl 1 ribbing for 4 [6, 6, 8] rows. Bind off loosely.

Repeat all steps for second sleeve.

Finishing

Weave in all loose ends to wrong side of work, and secure. Thread tapestry needle with 18″ (46cm) color D, and sew sleeves to bound-off stitches at underarm. Sew sleeve and side seams using mattress stitch. Rethread needle as needed.

To Rip or Not to Rip

If you realize you've made a mistake, you may decide to unravel some stitches or even many rows of your knitting. But keep in mind that some yarns, particularly chenille and novelty yarns, will not unravel well and may not be able to be reused. However, if you can rip out the yarn without damaging it, make absolutely sure to wind the yarn very loosely into a ball without stretching it. And as you put the stitches back on the needle, be careful not to twist them.

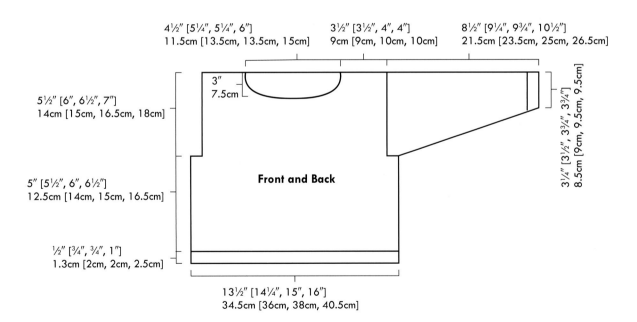

4½″ [5¼″, 5¼″, 6″]
11.5cm [13.5cm, 13.5cm, 15cm]

3½″ [3½″, 4″, 4″]
9cm [9cm, 10cm, 10cm]

8½″ [9¼″, 9¾″, 10½″]
21.5cm [23.5cm, 25cm, 26.5cm]

3″
7.5cm

3¼″ [3½″, 3¾″, 3¾″]
8.5cm [9cm, 9.5cm, 9.5cm]

5½″ [6″, 6½″, 7″]
14cm [15cm, 16.5cm, 18cm]

5″ [5½″, 6″, 6½″]
12.5cm [14cm, 15cm, 16.5cm]

Front and Back

½″ [¾″, ¾″, 1″]
1.3cm [2cm, 2cm, 2.5cm]

13½″ [14¼″, 15″, 16″]
34.5cm [36cm, 38cm, 40.5cm]

Dream Baby Hat and Cardigan

This baby sweater and hat truly are a dream to knit. Start off with the easy Dream Baby Hat, and move on to the cardigan to complete the set. Working the sweater from cuff to cuff, all in one piece, makes finishing a dream as well.

Designer: Beth Walker O'Brien

Size

Hat

0–6 months: 15″ (38cm) around,
7″ (18cm) tall

9 months: 16″ (40.5cm) around;
7½″ (19cm) tall

Cardigan

0–3 months: chest—19″ (48.5cm);
length—9″ (23cm)

3–6 months: chest—21″ (53.5cm);
length—10″ (25.5cm)

6–9 months: chest—23″ (58.5cm);
length—11″ (28cm)

⊛ ⊛ ⊛

Gauge

22 stitches/48 rows=4″ (10cm)
in garter stitch

⊛ ⊛ ⊛

What You'll Need

Yarn: DK weight machine-washable
baby yarn, hat and cardigan *each*:
about 245 yards [224m]/100g,
color A and color B

We used: King Cole Soft as Silk DK
(100% acrylic): #146 Ivory (color A),
1 skein for hat, 1 skein for cardigan;
#56 Cornflower (color B), 1 skein for
hat, 1 skein for cardigan

Needles: US size 5 (3.75mm)

Notions: Tapestry needle; 2 stitch
holders; sewing needle and thread to
match; 5 buttons ½″ (1.3cm) diameter
(for cardigan)

Note: Buttons and other small
objects may pose a choking hazard
for small children. Be sure to sew
buttons securely in place.

Note: Instructions are given for
smallest size; all other sizes are
listed in brackets. When only 1
number is given, it applies to all sizes.

Garter Stitch Pattern with Slip Stitch Selvedge

Row 1: (right side) With color A, knit
1 through back loop, knit across row until
1 stitch remains, with yarn in front slip
1 stitch purlwise. Turn work.
Row 2: (wrong side) Repeat row 1.
Row 3: With color B, knit 1 through back
loop, knit until 1 stitch remains, with yarn
in front slip 1 stitch purlwise. Turn work.
Row 4: Repeat row 3.

Techniques

Bar increase (page 18)
Binding off–BO (page 14)
Buttonholes (page 21)
Casting on–CO (page 9)
Garter stitch (page 15)
Knit 1 through back loop–k1tbl
(page 18)
Knit 2 together–k2tog (page 19)
Long tail cast-on (page 10)
Mattress stitch (page 23)
Slip slip knit decrease–ssk (page 19)
Slip stitches (page 16)
Yarn over–yo (page 17)

Make the hat

Front: Cast on 42 [45] stitches with color B. Work Garter Stitch with Slip Stitch Selvedge pattern for 7½″ [8″] (19cm [20.5cm]). End with wrong-side row. Bind off.

Back: Follow directions for hat front; start with color A instead of color B.

Finishing

With wrong sides facing up and pieces side-by-side, mattress stitch the front and back together along the slip stitch selvedge edge at the top of the hat. By mattress stitching from inside of hat, a decorative ridge is created on the outside. With right sides facing, seam sides of hat together using mattress stitch. Weave in remaining loose ends.

Make tassels: Wrap color B around 4 fingers about 20 times; cut yarn. Thread a short piece of color B through the loops, and tie an overhand knot at one end of yarn circle. Wrap another short piece of color B around yarn bunch, approximately 1″ (2.5cm) from top. Tie an overhand knot. Cut through bottom of loops; trim to even length.

Repeat all steps for second tassel.

Use yarn to sew tassels securely in place at corners of hat.

Make the cardigan

Make the left sleeve

With color B, cast on 34 [36, 38] stitches. Work Garter Stitch with Slip Stitch Selvedge pattern, increasing 1 stitch at each edge (see Note, next page) every 10 rows, 8 times. (50 [52, 54] stitches)

Note: Work all sleeve increase rows on right-side rows as follows: Knit 1 through back loop, knit into front loop then back loop of next stitch, knit across row until 3 stitches remain, knit into front loop then back loop of next stitch, knit 1, with yarn in front slip 1 stitch purlwise.

Work in pattern until sleeve measures 6¼″ [6¾″, 7¼″] (16cm [17cm, 18.5cm]) from cast-on edge, ending on wrong-side row. Do not bind off.

Make the body

With same color used on last row and beginning where yarn is still attached to knitting, cable cast on 25 [29, 33] stitches in front, and cut yarn, leaving 4″ (10cm) tail to weave in later (75 [81, 87] stitches). With same color and new length of yarn, cable cast on 25 [29, 33] stitches on other side of sweater, then cut yarn and leave 4″ (10cm) tail. (100 [110, 120] stitches)

With right sides of work facing and new color, work even in pattern as established for 2½″ [2¾″, 3″] (6.5cm [7cm, 7.5cm]), ending with wrong-side row.

Neck opening Divide for Front and Back as follows: Work in pattern for 50 [55, 60] stitches. Transfer remaining 50 [55, 60] stitches to stitch holder. (These will be the Left Center Front stitches.)

Center Back Work in pattern over 50 [55, 60] stitches for 4½″ [5″, 5½″] (11.5cm [12.5cm,14cm]), ending on wrong-side row. Transfer these stitches to another stitch holder. Cut yarns, leaving 4″ (10cm) tails.

Left Center Front Transfer the 50 [55, 60] Left Center Front stitches (from neck opening) from stitch holder to needle, and work in pattern for 2¼″ [2½″, 2¾″] (5.5cm [6.5cm, 7cm]), ending on wrong-side row. Work 4 more rows in pattern.

Buttonhole row (right side) Knit 1 through back loop, knit 2 [3, 3], *yarn over, knit 2 together, knit 9 [10, 11] stitches**; repeat from * to ** 3 times. Yarn over, knit 2 together, knit 7 [8, 9], knit 2 together, yarn over, knit

2 [2, 3], with yarn in front slip 1 stitch purlwise. Work 2 more rows in pattern, bind off on wrong side of work, and cut yarns. Weave in all loose ends to wrong side of work, and secure.

Right Center Front (separate piece) With same color used when binding off Left Center Front, use long tail cast-on method to cast on 50 [55, 60] stitches. Join the other color, and work 6 rows in pattern. Continue in pattern for another 2¼″ [2½″, 2¾″] (5.5cm [6.5cm, 7cm]), ending on wrong-side row. Leave stitches on needle and cut yarns, leaving 4″ (10cm) tails to weave in later.

Join Right Center Front to Back: Transfer the 50 [55, 60] Back stitches from stitch holder to the needle containing the Right Center Front stitches, making sure the Right Center Front stitches are to the left of the Back stitches when viewed from right side of work. Starting with right-side row and using the correct color to maintain pattern, join yarn and work in pattern across 100 [110, 120] stitches for 2½″ [2¾″, 3″] (6.5cm [7cm, 7.5cm]), ending on wrong-side row.

Make the right sleeve

With right side facing, bind off 25 [29, 33] stitches from body, knit 50 [52, 54], bind off 25 [29, 33] stitches. Cut yarn and pull through last stitch to secure. Rejoin yarn, and work in pattern for 50 [52, 54]

Button Up!

You don't have to purchase buttons at the beginning of a project. Instead, wait and take the finished project with you into the store. Try several different buttons in each of the buttonholes. You'll want to choose buttons that are consistent with your knitted fabric. A lightweight, loosely knit fabric may sag and pull out of shape with buttons that are too heavy, while dainty buttons will look out of place on a sturdy, bulky garment. (If your buttonholes are not identical, it's best to choose buttons that fit the smallest buttonhole. You can always tighten up the larger buttonholes with scrap yarn and a needle.)

stitches, decreasing 1 stitch at each edge of sleeve (see Note) every 10 rows, 8 times. (34 [36, 38] stitches)

Note: Work sleeve decrease rows on right-side rows as follows: Knit 1 through back loop, slip slip knit decrease, knit until 3 stitches left, knit 2 together, with yarn in front slip 1 stitch purlwise.

Work until sleeve measures 6¼″ [6¾″, 7¼″] (16cm [17cm, 18.5cm]) from body bind-off edge, ending

with right-side row. Bind off on wrong-side row. Cut yarns, leaving 4″ (10cm) tails.

Finishing

Using yarn and tapestry needle, seam sides together and close underarm seams with mattress stitch. Sew buttons to Right Center Front, aligning them with button-holes on Left Center Front. Weave in all loose ends to wrong sides, and secure. Block by placing dampened cloth over buttoned sweater; allow to dry.

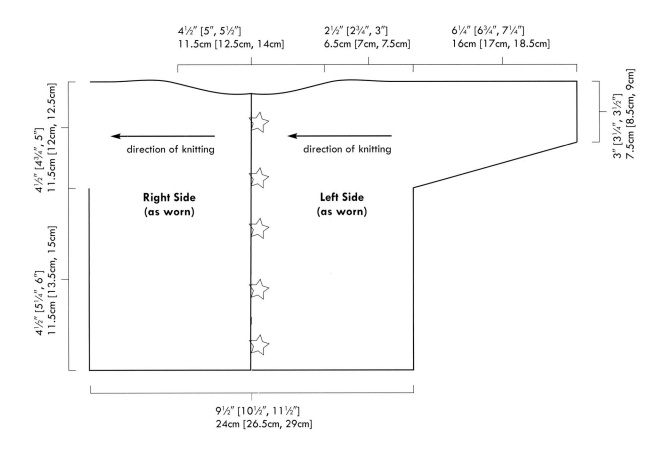

Trapeze Jacket and Muff 🧶 🧶

What little girl wouldn't love a mohair-trimmed jacket with matching muff?
This special outfit is sure to make her feel just like a snow princess.

Designer: Sharon Turner

Size

Jacket

2 years: chest—19″ (48.5cm); length—12½″ (31.5cm); sleeve length—10½″ (26.5cm)

3 years: chest—21″ (53.5cm); length—14″ (35.5cm); sleeve length—11¼″ (28.5cm)

4 years: chest—23″ (58.5cm); length—15½″ (39.6cm); sleeve length—12″ (30.5cm)

6 years: chest—25″ (63.5cm); length—17½″ (44.5cm); sleeve length—13″ (33cm)

⊗ ⊗ ⊗

Gauge

16 stitches/20 rows=4″ (10cm) in stockinette stitch on size 9 (5.5mm) needles

⊗ ⊗ ⊗

What You'll Need

Yarn: 508 [508, 635, 762] yards (465m [465m, 519m, 646m]) heavy worsted weight yarn (50% wool, 50% llama), yarn A; 248 [248, 248, 330] yards (247m [247m, 247m, 330m]) bulky weight yarn (80% mohair, 20% wool), yarn B

We used: Classic Elite Montera (50% wool, 50% llama blend): #093 blue (yarn A), 4 [4, 5, 6] skeins; Classic Elite La Gran Mohair (77% mohair, 17% wool, 6% nylon): #6501 white (yarn B), 2 [2, 2, 3] balls

Needles: US size 9 (5.5mm); US size 9 (5.5mm) double-pointed; US size 8 (5mm)

Notions: Stitch holders; tapestry needle; steam iron; straight pins; piece cardboard; 3 large (size 4) sew-on snaps; size I/9 (5.5mm) crochet hook

Note: Instructions are given for smallest size; all other sizes are in brackets. When only 1 number is given, it applies to all sizes.

Make the jacket

Make the back: Using size 9 (5.5mm) straight needles and yarn B, cast on 76 [82, 90, 100] stitches. Work in stockinette stitch for 2″ (5cm), ending with wrong-side row and decreasing 8 [10, 12, 14] stitches evenly across last row. (68 [72, 78, 86] stitches)

Change to yarn A. Work in stockinette stitch, decreasing 1 stitch at each end of needle every 5th row 6 [6, 7, 9] times (56 [60, 64, 68] stitches). Work even until back measures 5″ [6″, 7″, 8½″] (12.5cm [15cm, 18cm, 21.5cm]) from beginning of yarn A.

Shape the armhole Continuing in stockinette stitch, bind off 4 stitches at beginning of next 2 rows, then bind off 1 stitch at beginning of next 10 rows (38 [42, 46, 50] stitches). Work even until armhole measures 6½″ [7″, 7½″, 8″] (16.5cm [18cm, 19cm, 20.5cm]).

Next row: Work 9 [10, 12, 13] stitches, place on stitch holder for later. Bind off center 20 [22, 22, 24] stitches for back neck. Work remaining 9 [10, 12, 13] stitches, place on stitch holder for later.

Make the left front: With size 9 (5.5mm) straight needles and yarn B, cast on 43 [46, 50, 54] stitches. Work in stockinette stitch for 2″ (5cm), ending with wrong-side row and decreasing 6 [7, 8, 8] stitches evenly across last row. (37 [39, 42, 46])

Change to yarn A.

Shape the side edge Beginning with a knit row, work in stockinette stitch, decreasing 1 stitch on left side edge every 5th row 6 [6, 7, 9] times (31 [33, 35, 37] stitches). Work even until left front measures 5″ [6″, 7″, 8½″] (12.5cm [15cm, 18cm, 21.5cm]) from beginning of yarn A, ending with wrong-side row.

Shape the armhole Bind off 4 stitches; knit to end of row. Bind off 1 stitch at beginning of every right-side row 5 times (22 [24, 26, 28] stitches). Work even without further shaping until left front measures

Techniques

Binding off—BO (page 14)

Casting on—CO (page 9)

Crochet chain (page 26)

Garter stitch (page 15)

Knit into front and back loops (page 18)

Knit 2 together–k2tog (page 19)

Make 1 increase—m1 (page 18)

Purl 2 together–p2tog (page 19)

Reverse stockinette stitch (page 15)

Slip slip knit decrease—ssk (page 19)

Stockinette stitch—St st (page 15)

Three-needle bind-off (page 24)

9″ [10½″, 12″, 14″] (23cm [26.5cm, 30.5cm, 35.5cm]) from beginning of yarn A, ending with right-side row.

Shape the neck Bind off 7 [7, 7, 8] stitches at beginning of row (neck edge); purl to end of row. Work 1 row even. Bind off 3 stitches at beginning of next row (neck edge), purl to end of row. Work 1 row even. Now bind off 1 stitch at neck edge *every other* row 3 [4, 4, 4] times (9 [10, 12, 13] stitches). Work even until piece measures same as back, placing remaining 9 [10, 12, 13] stitches on a stitch holder. Cut yarn, leaving 20″ (51cm) tail with which to seam shoulder together later.

Make the right front: Work same as left front, reversing side, armhole, and neck shaping. This means that when working the side edge, make all decreases on right-side edge of garment. Continue same as left front until it's time to shape armhole; make all bind-offs on wrong-side rows for all armhole shaping. Work same as left front until it's time to shape neck; make all neck bind-offs on right-side rows.

Make the sleeves: With size 9 (5.5mm) straight needles and yarn B, cast on 40 [42, 42, 45] stitches. Work in stockinette stitch for 1½″ (3.8cm), ending with wrong-side row and decreasing 6 [6, 6, 7] stitches evenly across last row (34 [36, 36, 38] stitches). Change to yarn A, and beginning with a knit row, work 2 rows even in stockinette stitch. Still working in stockinette, increase 1 stitch at each end of next row, then each end of *every other* row 1 [0, 3, 3] times, then every 4th row 7 [9, 8, 9] times (52 [56, 60, 64] stitches). Work even until sleeve measures 7¾″ [8½″, 9¼″, 10¼″] (19.5cm [21.5cm, 23.5cm, 26cm]) from beginning of yarn A.

Shape the cap Bind off 4 stitches at beginning of next 2 rows, then bind off 1 stitch at beginning of next 10 rows (34 [38, 42, 46] stitches). Work 1 row even, then bind off all stitches.

Repeat all steps for second sleeve.

Make the collar: The collar is worked entirely in garter stitch with yarn B. With size 9 (5.5mm) straight needles and yarn B, cast on 44 [46, 46, 52] stitches. Knit 1 row.

Next row: Knit 1, make 1, knit across row until 1 stitch remains, make 1, knit 1. (46 [48, 48, 54] stitches)

Repeat increase row 2 times, then repeat increase row *every other* row 2 times (54 [56, 56, 62] stitches). Work collar without further shaping until it measures 2½″ [2½″, 3″, 3¼″] (6.5cm [6.5cm, 7.5cm, 8.5cm]) from beginning. Bind off.

Finishing

Weave in loose ends to wrong side of work. Lightly steam pieces, excluding mohair trim and collar.

Finish shoulder seams: Slip shoulder stitches from holders onto size 9 (5.5mm) double-pointed needles, and with yarn attached to shoulder stitches, join left front and back shoulder stitches together using three-needle bind-off. Cut yarn; pull through last stitch to secure. Repeat for right shoulder. Lightly steam shoulder seams.

Attach sleeves and collar: With right sides facing each other, pin sleeve caps to armholes, matching up bound-off stitches of sleeve to bound-off stitches of armhole. Backstitch in place. Sew inside sleeve seams and side seams, reversing seams for rolled mohair trim. With right side of collar facing wrong side of jacket, center collar at back neck; pin to neckline. Stitch collar in place using backstitch; turn collar down when finished. Lightly steam seams, avoiding mohair. Remove all pins.

Make pom-poms: Make 3 pom-poms (see next page). Sew 1 pom-pom to right front neck edge. Attach next pom-pom ½″ (1″, 1½″, 2″) (1.3cm [2.5cm, 3.8cm, 5cm]) above where mohair trim meets yarn A on right front. Center last pom-pom between these 2; sew in place.

Add snaps: Sew the top half of the snaps to the underside of right front under pom-poms,

½″ (1.3cm) in from edge. Sew bottom half of snaps on top of left front, matching the snap tops.

Make the muff

With size 9 (5.5mm) straight needles and yarn B, cast on 45 stitches. Work in stockinette stitch for 4″ (10cm), ending with wrong-side row. *Purl next row (right side), and knit following (wrong side) row**. Repeat from * to ** 2 times for a total of 6 rows. Change to yarn A. Beginning with a knit row (right side), work in stockinette stitch until piece measures 7″ (18cm) from beginning of yarn A. End with wrong-side row. Change to yarn B; knit 1 row. *Knit next row (wrong side), and purl following row (right side)**. Repeat from * to ** 2 times for a total of 6 rows.

Next row: (wrong side) Purl.

Work in stockinette stitch until piece measures 5″ (12.5cm) from end of yarn A section. Bind off all stitches.

Finishing

Lightly steam yarn A section of knitted piece. Fold muff in half lengthwise with right sides facing, and sew long edges together. Leaving piece inside out, roll mohair panels back at each end so cast-on edge and bind-off edge touch. Stitch the 2 edges together all the way around the center. Turn muff right side out

so that yarn A is on the outside, with reverse stockinette stitch yarn B trim at side edges.

Make the neck strap: Cut 3 strands of yarn A 6 times longer than you want the strap to be. Hold the strands together, and work a crochet chain to the ends. Sew ends of chain to top of muff corners where yarn A meets yarn B. Make a pom-pom the same size as for jacket, and sew to center front of muff.

The Knitty-Gritty

Making Pom-Poms

Cut 2 circles out of cardboard, each about 3″ (7.5cm) in diameter. Cut a small hole in the center of each circle; make a slit from the outside edge of both circles to the center holes.

Hold both circles together, with the slits aligned. Wind the yarn evenly around both circles (going through the slits to the center holes) as tightly as possible, about 50 to 100 times. (The more times you wrap, the fuller the pom-pom will be). When the circles are fully covered, cut the yarn around the outer edges of the circles. Cut one 18″ (46cm) strand of yarn and, pulling the cardboard circles apart very slightly, wrap the strand yarn firmly around the yarn centers a couple of times. Tie the strand tightly in a double knot. Remove the cardboard circles completely, and fluff out the pom-pom. Trim ends to even out if necessary.

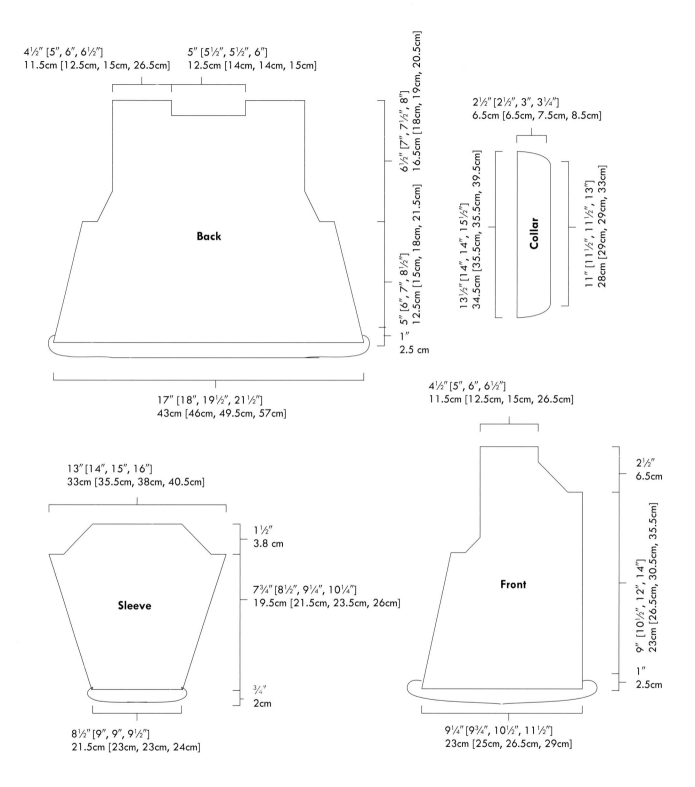

4½″ [5″, 6″, 6½″]
11.5cm [12.5cm, 15cm, 26.5cm]

5″ [5½″, 5½″, 6″]
12.5cm [14cm, 14cm, 15cm]

6½″ [7″, 7½″, 8″] 16.5cm [18cm, 19cm, 20.5cm]

Back

5″ [6″, 7″, 8½″] 12.5cm [15cm, 18cm, 21.5cm]

1″
2.5 cm

17″ [18″, 19½″, 21½″]
43cm [46cm, 49.5cm, 57cm]

2½″ [2½″, 3″, 3¼″]
6.5cm [6.5cm, 7.5cm, 8.5cm]

13½″ [14″, 14″, 15½″] 34.5cm [35.5cm, 35.5cm, 39.5cm]

Collar

11″ [11½″, 11½″, 13″] 28cm [29cm, 29cm, 33cm]

13″ [14″, 15″, 16″]
33cm [35.5cm, 38cm, 40.5cm]

1½″
3.8 cm

Sleeve

7¾″ [8½″, 9¼″, 10¼″]
19.5cm [21.5cm, 23.5cm, 26cm]

¾″
2cm

8½″ [9″, 9″, 9½″]
21.5cm [23cm, 23cm, 24cm]

4½″ [5″, 6″, 6½″]
11.5cm [12.5cm, 15cm, 26.5cm]

2½″
6.5cm

Front

9″ [10½″, 12″, 14″] 23cm [26.5cm, 30.5cm, 35.5cm]

1″
2.5cm

9¼″ [9¾″, 10½″, 11½″]
23cm [25cm, 26.5cm, 29cm]

Striped Overalls

This unisex cotton romper is about the cutest thing you've ever seen! Knit in bold stripes and even bolder colors, it's an attention-grabber that's sure to turn heads. Toddlers can wear it long (to the ankles) or slightly shorter for a funkier look.

Designer: Sharon Turner

Size

6–12 months: finished chest—21¾" (55cm); length—19½" (49.5cm)

12–18 months: finished chest—22½" (57cm); length—21¾" (55cm)

2 years: finished chest—24" (61cm); length—23½" (59.5cm)

3 years: finished chest—24¾" (63cm); length—25½" (65cm)

Gauge

22 stitches/28 rows=4" (10cm) in stockinette stitch on size 6 (4mm) needles

What You'll Need

Yarn: 100% cotton worsted weight yarn: 324 [432, 432, 432] yards (296m [395m, 395m, 395m]) color A; 216 [216, 216, 324] yards (198m [181m, 181m, 296m]) color B; 108 yards (99m) color C

We used: Tahki Cotton Classic (100% mercerized cotton): #3873 blue (color A), 3 [4, 4, 4] skeins; #3726 lime green (color B), 2 [2, 2, 3] skeins; #3424 (color C), 1 skein

Needles: US size 3 (3.25mm); US size 6 (4mm); US size 6 (4mm) circular, 24" (60cm) long

Notions: 2 stitch holders; stitch marker; iron and ironing board; straight pins; tapestry needle; sewing needle and thread to match; 6 buttons, ⅝" (1.5cm) in diameter (optional); 4 buttons, ⅞" (2.2cm) in diameter

Note: Instructions are given for smallest size; larger sizes are listed in brackets. When only 1 number is given, it applies to all sizes.

Stripe Pattern

Work 6 [7, 8, 9] rows in stockinette stitch using color B, then 6 [7, 8, 9] rows with color A.

Techniques

Binding off–BO (page 14)
Buttonholes (page 21)
Casting on–CO (page 9)
Garter stitch (page 15)
Knit 2 together–k2tog (page 19)
Picking up stitches (page 22)
Stockinette stitch–St st (page 15)
Yarn over–yo (page 17)

Make the legs

With size 3 needles and color A, cast on 82 [85, 88, 91] stitches. Work in garter stitch for ¾" [1", 1", 1"] (2cm [2.5cm, 2.5cm, 2.5cm]), ending with wrong-side row. Change to size 6 straight needles and color B. Beginning with knit row, work Stripe Pattern for 6 stripes above garter stitch cuff, ending with full stripe in color A.

Crotch: Maintaining Stripe Pattern, bind off 3 stitches at beginning of next 2 rows, then bind off 1 stitch at beginning of next 4 rows. Finish with full stripe in color B. Place remaining 72 [75, 78, 81] stitches on stitch holder.

Repeat all steps for other leg.

Make the body

Slip stitches from both legs onto circular needle (144 [150, 156, 162] stitches). With right side facing and color A, join stitches into a circle and place stitch marker at beginning of round to mark as center back. Knit every round, maintaining Stripe Pattern, for 5 more stripes (12 stripes total above garter stitch cuff).

With color B, work 13th stripe as follows: Knit 2 [2, 2, 3] rounds even. On the 3rd [3rd, 3rd, 4th] round, work as follows: *Knit 22 [23, 24, 25], knit 2 together**; work from * to ** 6 times (138 [144, 150, 156] stitches). On the 4th [4th, 4th, 5th] round, *knit 21 [22, 23, 24], knit 2 together**; work from * to ** 6 times (132 [138, 144, 150] stitches). On the 5th [5th, 5th, 6th] round, *knit 20 [21, 22, 23], knit 2 together** 6 times (126 [132, 138, 144] stitches). Work the 6th [6th, 6th, 7th] round

as *knit 19 [20, 21, 22], knit 2 together** 6 times (120 [126, 132, 138] stitches). Work even for next 0 [1, 2, 2] rounds to complete stripe.

12–18 month and 3-year sizes: Change to color A; work 2 more rounds, decreasing in round 2 as follows: *Knit 40 [44], knit 2 together** 2 times, knit to end. (124 [136] stitches)

6-month and 2-year sizes: Knit 2 more rounds even. (120 [132] stitches)

Make the bodice

Slip first 30 [31, 33, 34] stitches onto size 6 straight needle. Place 60 [62, 66, 68] stitches on stitch holder, and slip last 30 [31, 33, 34] stitches onto same size 6 needle as the first group of stitches.

Back: Working flat and beginning with knit row, work 14 rows of stockinette stitch with color A. Bind off 8 stitches at beginning of next 2 rows. Work even with color A over 44 [46, 50, 52] stitches until back measures 6″ [6¼″, 6¼″, 6¼″] (15cm [16cm, 16cm, 16cm]) from end of last color B stripe, ending with wrong-side row.

Straps: Knit 10 stitches for first strap. Join second ball of color A, bind off center 24 [26, 30, 32] stitches, knit remaining 10 stitches for second strap. Work both shoulder straps at same time:
Row 1: (wrong side) Purl.
Row 2: (right side) Decrease 1 stitch at neck edges of each strap. (9 stitches each strap)

Repeat rows 1 and 2 (8 stitches each strap). Purl 1 row. Change to size 3 needles; work in garter stitch for 3¾″ [3¾″, 3¼″, 3¼″] (9.5cm [9.5cm, 8.5cm, 8.5cm]).

Buttonhole row On each strap, knit 3, yarn over, knit 2 together, knit 3. Work 1″ (2.5cm) more in garter stitch. Bind off strap stitches.

Front: Slip the 60 [62, 66, 68] stitches from holder onto size 6 straight needles. Beginning with right-side row, work in stockinette stitch for 10 rows.

Make side buttonholes Knit 4, knit 2 together, yarn over, work across row to last 6 stitches, yarn over, knit 2 together, knit 4. Work 3 more rows in stockinette stitch. Bind off 8 stitches at beginning of next 2 rows. Work even over 44 [46, 50, 52] stitches until front measures 3½″ [3½″, 4″, 4″] (9cm [9cm, 10cm, 10cm]) from end of last color B stripe. Change to size 3 needles, and work in garter stitch for 1″ (2.5cm). Bind off all stitches.

Make the pockets

Note: Before picking up pocket stitches, lay overalls flat on ironing board, cover with a light cloth, and lightly steam-press entire garment.

Weave size 3 needle under and over stitches to pick up 30 [30, 32, 32] stitches about 7¼″ [7¼″, 7½″, 7½″] (18.5cm [18.5cm, 19cm, 19cm]) down from the division of front and back bodice and centered on side of pant leg. With size 6 needles and color C, work the picked-up stitches in stockinette stitch until pocket measures 4″ [4″, 4¼″, 4¼″] (10cm [10cm, 11cm, 11cm]), ending with right-side row. Work 3 rows in garter stitch to prevent pocket top from curling. Bind off all pocket stitches. Steam-press pockets; pin sides in place. Thread tapestry needle with 18″ (46cm) color C, and sew pocket sides to pant legs.

Repeat for second pocket.

Make the button bands

Note: If you don't want button bands along the inside legs, simply sew inside leg seams together using mattress stitch, and skip ahead to finishing.

Sew crotch seams together. Weave in loose ends along inner leg edges.

Beginning at bottom of back left leg cuff, using size 3 needles and color A and with right side facing, pick up and knit 28 [35, 42, 49] stitches up leg to crotch seam and another 28 [35, 42, 49] stitches down right back leg to bottom of cuff (56 [70, 84, 98] stitches). (This works out to about 4 [5, 6, 7] stitches along each stripe, including cuff.)

Rows 1 and 2: Knit.

Row 3: Knit 5 [5, 6, 7] stitches, purl to last 5 [5, 6, 7] stitches, knit to end of row.

Row 4: Knit.

Row 5: Repeat row 3.

Rows 6–7: Knit.

Bind off.

Buttonhole band: Work as for button band, picking up 56 [70, 84, 98] stitches from bottom of cuff on right front leg around to bottom of cuff on left front leg.

Row 1 and 2: Knit.

Row 3: Knit 5 [5, 6, 7] stitches, purl to last 5 [5, 6, 7] stitches, knit to end of row.

Row 4: Knit 9 [11, 14, 16], yarn over, knit 2 together, *knit 6 [8, 10, 12], yarn over, knit 2 together**; repeat from * to ** once, knit 3 [4, 4, 6], yarn over, knit 2 together, *knit 6 [8, 10, 12], yarn over, knit 2 together**; repeat from * to ** once, knit remaining 8 [11, 14, 16] stitches.

Row 5: Repeat row 3.

Rows 6–7: Knit.

Bind off.

Finishing

Use matching thread to attach buttons, or cut a few strands of color B, about 15–20″ (38–51cm) long, and separate the 5-ply yarn to use as thread. If you made the button band on inner legs, sew 6 buttons opposite the buttonholes. Button the bands closed to hold legs in place, and sew together garter stitch cuff corners, keeping them overlapped same as button bands. Sew the 4 larger buttons opposite buttonholes on bodice. Weave in all loose ends to wrong side, and secure.

You Expect Me to Knit All That?

Do you choose your knitting projects based on which one has the shortest instructions? Most of us think "oh, this has a short pattern, so it must be easy." But don't let the length of a pattern keep you from making something you really love. You may find that a challenging pattern is even more fun to tackle than something simple.

Start out by making a swatch with the same yarn you will use for the pattern. Do you like the way it looks and feels? If you do, work the instructions one stitch at a time, use markers between pattern repeats if you need to, and use a row counter to help you keep your place. Before you know it, you'll have created something spectacular.

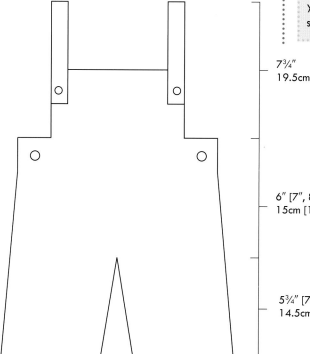

7¾″
19.5cm

6″ [7″, 8″, 9″]
15cm [18cm, 20.5cm, 23cm]

5¾″ [7″, 7¾″, 8¾″]
14.5cm [18cm, 19.5cm, 22cm]

CHAPTER 4

Classic Garments

Ah, the appeal of a hand-knit sweater. Snuggly, ruffly, sporty, simple … you'll find all kinds of appealing garments in this chapter. Even novice knitters can make a sweater—there's no reason to feel intimidated. Just read the instructions beforehand, and get started.

Ribbon Tank Top

This is a perfect project to tackle as your first handknit garment. Learn basic shaping techniques while making this stunning summer tank top. The ribbon yarn adds an interesting touch to a very simple shape.

Designer: Beth Walker O'Brien

Techniques

Backstitch (page 23)
Binding off—BO (page 14)
Blocking (page 27)
Casting on—CO (page 9)
Decreases—dec (page 19)
Garter stitch (page 15)
Increases—inc (page 17)
Stockinette stitch—St st (page 15)

Sizes

Extra small: blocked chest—34″ (86.5cm) in circumference, 19″ (48.5cm) in length

Small: blocked chest—36″ (91.5cm) in circumference, 20″ (51cm) in length

Medium: blocked chest 38″ (96.5cm) in circumference, 21″ (53.5cm) in length

Large: blocked chest—40″ (101.5cm) in circumference, 22″ (56cm) in length

Gauge

19 stitches/23 rows=4″ (10cm) (unblocked)
18 stitches/22 rows=4″ (10cm) (blocked)

What You'll Need

Yarn: 800 yards variegated ribbon worsted weight yarn

We used: Berroco Zen Colors (55% cotton, 45% nylon): #8108 Raku, 7 skeins

Needles: US size 7 (4.5mm), US size 9 (5.5mm)

Notions: Tapestry needle; sewing needle and thread to match (optional)

Note: Instructions are given for smallest size; all other sizes are in brackets. When only 1 number or set of instructions is given, it applies to all sizes.

Make the back

With size 7 needles, cast on 76 [80, 86, 90] stitches. Work in garter stitch for 6 rows. Change to size 9 needles, and work in stockinette stitch until piece measures 9″ [10″, 10½″, 11″] (23cm [25.5cm, 26.5cm, 28cm]) from cast-on edge.

Shape the armhole: Bind off 7 [7, 8, 8] stitches at beginning of next 2 rows (62 [66, 70, 74] stitches). Beginning with next row, decrease 1 stitch at each side edge, then decrease at each side edge every other row, for a total of 7 times (48 [52, 56, 60] stitches). Work in stockinette stitch until piece measures 15″ [16″, 16½″, 17½″] (38cm [40.5cm, 42cm, 44.5cm]), ending with wrong-side row.

Shape the neck: Knit 9 [10, 11, 12] stitches, attach another ball of yarn, bind off center 30 [32, 34, 36] stitches, and knit to end of row. In the following rows, decrease 1 stitch at each neck edge every other row 3 [4, 5, 6] times (6 stitches remain on each shoulder). Continue in stockinette stitch until piece measures 17″ [18″, 19″, 20″] (43cm [46cm, 48.5cm, 51cm]) from cast-on edge. Bind off.

Make the front

Work same as back until piece measures 12″ [13½″, 14″, 15″] (30.5cm [34.5cm, 35.5cm, 38cm]), ending with wrong-side row.

Shape the neck: Knit 15 [16, 16, 17] stitches, attach another ball of yarn, bind off center 18 [20, 24, 26] stitches, and knit to end of row. Working both sides at the same time, decrease 1 stitch at each neck edge, every other row 9 [10, 10, 11] times (6 stitches remain on each shoulder). Continue in stockinette stitch until piece measures 17″ [18″, 19″, 20″] (43cm [46cm, 48.5cm, 51cm]). Bind off.

Finishing

Sew side seams together using backstitch. Pick up about 82 [82, 86, 90] stitches around an armhole edge, and knit 4 rows. Bind off. Repeat for other armhole. Sew 1 shoulder seam. Pick up about 120 [124, 128, 136] stitches around neck edge, and knit 4 rows. Bind off. Sew other shoulder seam. Weave in all loose ends to wrong side of work; weave through several stitches to secure.

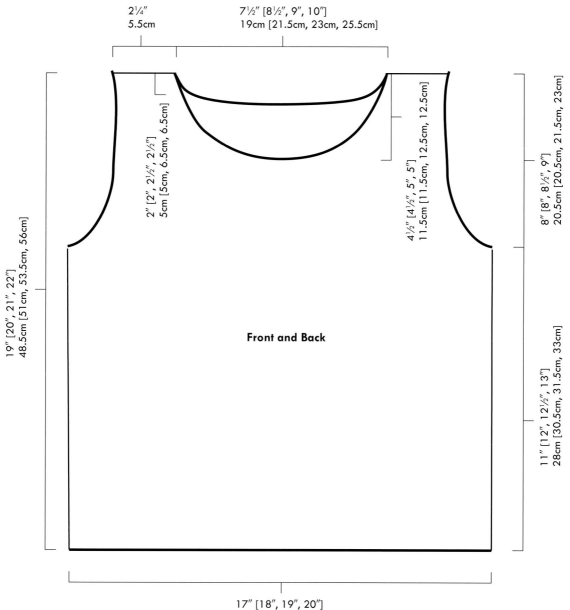

2¼"
5.5cm

7½" [8½", 9", 10"]
19cm [21.5cm, 23cm, 25.5cm]

2" [2", 2½", 2½"]
5cm [5cm, 6.5cm, 6.5cm]

4½" [4½", 5", 5"]
11.5cm [11.5cm, 12.5cm, 12.5cm]

8" [8", 8½", 9"]
20.5cm [20.5cm, 21.5cm, 23cm]

19" [20", 21", 22"]
48.5cm [51cm, 53.5cm, 56cm]

Front and Back

11" [12", 12½", 13"]
28cm [30.5cm, 31.5cm, 33cm]

17" [18", 19", 20"]
43cm [46cm, 48.5cm, 51cm]

Slip Slidin' Away

Ribbon yarns are usually slippery, so consider using sewing thread and a sewing needle to tack down the yarn ends to prevent them from slipping through to the right side of the garment.

Another thing to remember about ribbon yarns is that they have a tendency to stretch when worn. The instructions and measurements for this project are written with this in mind. Therefore, the knitted pieces will be smaller than the finished and blocked measurements. Block each piece to size as shown above.

Linen Pullover

Linen yarn knits up into a delicate, lovely fabric, especially when knit on large needles. The subtle texture accentuates the classic design of this sweater, which is knit all in one piece from cuff to cuff.

Designer: Amy Merritt

Techniques
Backstitch (page 23)
Binding off–BO (page 14)
Casting on–CO (page 9)
Joining circular knitting (page 16)
Stockinette stitch–St st (page 15)

Size
Chest: 32″–44″ (81.5cm–112cm), length: 25″ (63.5cm)

Gauge
16 stitches/16 rows=4″ (10cm) in circular stockinette stitch

What You'll Need
Yarn: 1,040 yards (951m) linen 4-ply yarn
We used: Euroflax 4-ply Linen (100% linen): #2 tobacco, 4 skeins

Needles: 2 US size 10 (6mm) circular: 16″ (40.5cm) long, 24″ (61cm) long

Notions: Stitch marker; 2 stitch holders; tapestry needle

Note: Work is very loose; take all measurements with fabric stretched slightly lengthwise.

Make the pullover

Beginning at cuff and using 16″ circular needles, loosely cast on 48 stitches. Join stitches into a circle, being careful not to twist cast-on stitches. Place marker between last and first stitches to mark beginning of round, and slide marker from left to right needle at beginning of each subsequent round. Work in circular stockinette stitch (knit each round) until sleeve measures 20″ (51cm) or desired length from cast-on edge to underarm. Change from circular stockinette stitch to flat, back-and-forth stockinette stitch (knit 1 row, purl 1 row), and loosely cast on 52 stitches at the end of each of the next 2 rows, switching to 24″ circular needles when needed (152 stitches). **Note:** For a longer sweater, add 4 stitches on each side for every extra inch in length, and don't forget to buy at least 1 more skein of yarn.

Work back and forth in regular stockinette stitch (knit 1 row, purl 1 row) over all stitches until work measures 5½″ (14cm) from beginning of body cast-on stitches.

Make neck opening: On next right-side row, knit across half the stitches (76 stitches); place remaining 76 stitches on stitch holder. Turn work, and purl 76 stitches. Continue working in stockinette stitch over 76 stitches until piece measures 11″ (28cm) from beginning of neck opening. Place these 76 stitches onto another stitch holder. Put the 76 stitches from first stitch holder onto circular needle, and work in stockinette stitch for 11″ (28cm) to match first half.

Join both halves together: On next row, when you reach neck opening, slip stitches from holder back onto circular needle with the other stitches, and continue working across row to close neck opening. Work even in stockinette stitch on all 152 stitches until piece measures 5½″ (14cm) from neck closing. At beginning of each of next 2 rows, loosely bind off 52 stitches. (48 stitches)

Change to 16″ circular needles, and work in circular stockinette stitch (knit every round) on 48 stitches until sleeve measures 20″ (51cm) or same length as first sleeve. Bind off loosely.

Finishing

With yarn threaded on tapestry needle, sew side seams together using backstitch. Weave in all loose ends to wrong side, and secure by weaving through stitches or along seam edges. Wash pullover, block to size. (Note: Euroflax linen can be machine-washed on delicate cycle and machine-dried at lowest heat setting.)

Loosen Up

Linen yarn softens and becomes more pliable with each wash. If the yarn feels too stiff before knitting, tie the skein in 4 places with short pieces of yarn to secure the strands so they won't tangle. Wash in warm, soapy water, rinse well, and dry. When the yarn is dry, remove the ties, wind the skein into a ball, and begin knitting.

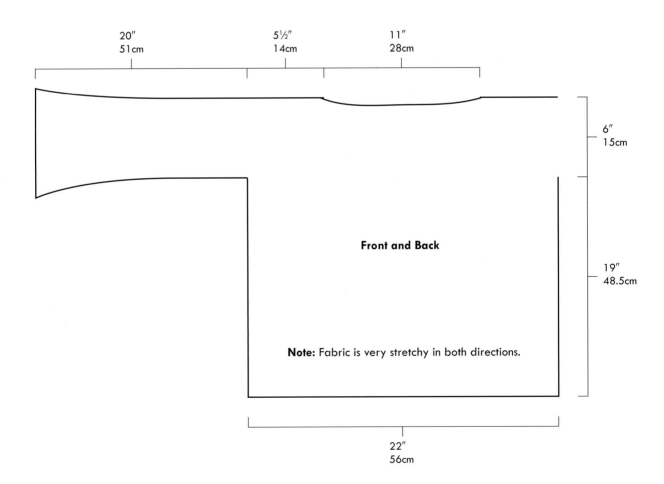

20″
51cm

5½″
14cm

11″
28cm

6″
15cm

Front and Back

19″
48.5cm

Note: Fabric is very stretchy in both directions.

22″
56cm

Simply Snuggly Turtleneck

A snuggly, cozy turtleneck sweater that can be made by a beginning knitter: What more could you ask for to get you through a long, cold winter?　　　Designer: Needful Yarns Design Studio

Techniques

Backstitch (page 23)

Binding off—BO (page 14)

Casting on—CO (page 9)

Increases—inc (page 17)

Reverse stockinette stitch (page 13)

Stockinette stitch—St st (page 15)

Sizes

Small: bust—35½″ (90cm); length from shoulder—21½″ (54.5cm); sleeve length to underarm—16½″ (42cm)

Medium: bust—40½″ (103cm); length from shoulder—24″ (61cm); sleeve length to underarm—17½″ (44.5cm)

Gauge

11 stitches/16 rows=4″ (10cm)

What You'll Need

Yarn: 585 [819] yards (535m [749m]) bulky weight blended yarn

We used: Filtes Van Dyck (46% wool, 39% acrylic, 15% alpaca): #120, 5 [7] balls

Needles: US size 11 (8mm)

Notions: Tapestry needle; long sewing pins with colored heads

---

Note: Instructions are given for smaller size; larger size is in brackets. When only 1 number or set of instructions is given, it applies to both sizes.

Make the back

Cast on 50 [56] stitches. Beginning with wrong-side (purl) row, work in stockinette stitch until piece measures 14″ [15″] (35.5cm [38cm]). End with wrong-side row.

Shape armhole

Row 1: (right side) Bind off 3 stitches, knit to end of row.

Row 2: (wrong side) Bind off 3 stitches, purl to end of row.

Row 3: Bind off 2 stitches, knit to end of row.

Row 4: Bind off 2 stitches, purl to end of row.

Row 5: Bind off 1 stitch, knit to end of row.

Row 6: Bind off 1 stitch, purl to end of row. (38 [44] stitches)

Continue in stockinette stitch until armhole measures 7½″ [9″] (19cm [23cm]), ending with wrong-side row.

Shape shoulder and collar: Bind off 7 stitches at beginning of next row, knit to end of row. Bind off 7 stitches at beginning of next row, purl to end of row. (24 [30] stitches)

Note: The collar is worked in reverse stockinette stitch so when it's turned over, the knit side will be visible and will match the rest of the sweater.

Next row: (right side) Purl.

Next row: (wrong side) Knit.

Continue in reverse stockinette stitch until collar measures 7½″ [19cm]. Bind off all stitches loosely.

Front of sweater

Work front the same as sweater back.

The Shop Around the Corner

Your local yarn shop is a fabulous resource! You'll be welcomed by friendly people who are eager for you to succeed in all that you knit. The best owners are knowledgeable, patient people who will make sure you get off to the right start. They'll help you choose the right yarn for your project, and they'll recommend patterns that fit your skill level. They seem to go the extra mile to make you a contented knitter. A yarn shop also can be a great place to make new friends who share your love of knitting.

Make the sleeves

Cast on 22 [26] stitches. Beginning with wrong-side (purl) row, work in stockinette stitch for 2″ (5cm). End with wrong-side row.

Shape sleeve: Continue with stockinette stitch, increasing 1 stitch at the beginning and end of next knit row, then every 6th row thereafter for a total of 6 times (34 [38] stitches). Work even without further increases until sleeve measures 16½″ [17½″] (42cm [44.5cm]), ending with wrong-side row.

Shape cap: Bind off 3 stitches at beginning of next 2 rows (28 [32] stitches). Work 1 row even. Bind off 2 stitches at beginning of next 2 rows (24 [28] stitches). Work 1 row even. Bind off 1 stitch at begin-

ning and end of next row, then every 4th row, 4 times (14 [18] stitches). Work even for 3 rows. Bind off 2 stitches at beginning of next 2 [4] rows. Bind off remaining 10 stitches.

Finishing

Block pieces lightly to size. Using backstitch for all seams, work as follows: With right sides together and using tapestry needle threaded with matching yarn, sew shoulder and collar seams. Rethread needle as necessary. Ease sleeve caps into armholes, pin in place, then sew. Sew sides and sleeve seams. With tapestry needle, weave in all loose ends to wrong side of work and through several stitches to secure. Turn collar to right side at halfway.

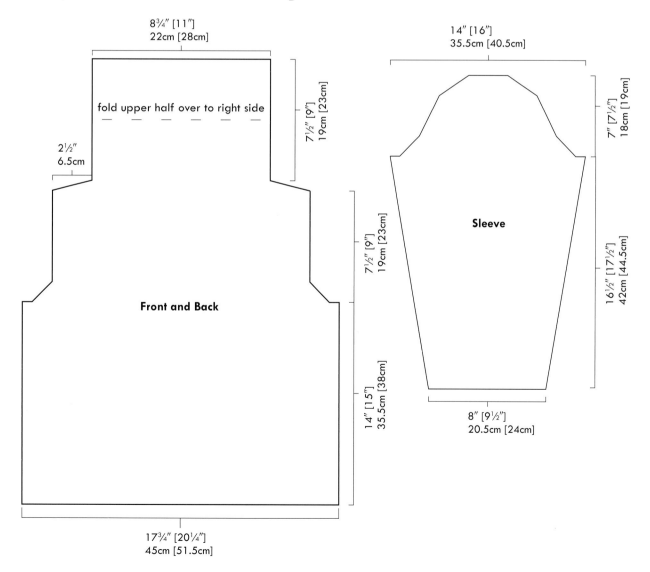

8¾″ [11″]
22cm [28cm]

fold upper half over to right side

7½″ [9″]
19cm [23cm]

2½″
6.5cm

Front and Back

7½″ [9″]
19cm [23cm]

14″ [15″]
35.5cm [38cm]

17¾″ [20¼″]
45cm [51.5cm]

14″ [16″]
35.5cm [40.5cm]

7″ [7½″]
18cm [19cm]

Sleeve

16½″ [17½″]
42cm [44.5cm]

8″ [9½″]
20.5cm [24cm]

Ruffly Cardigan

A hip alternative to the classic buttoned-up cardigan, this stunning lime sweater is a real head-turner. With shocking green yarn and fun ruffly detail, it's anything but ordinary. It's knit from cuff to cuff so the grain of the work goes sideways for yet another unexpected twist!

Designer: Jessica Peterson

Techniques
Binding off—BO (page 14)
Casting on—CO (page 9)
Double crochet—dc, (page 26)
Knit 2 together—k2tog (page 19)
Make 1 increase—m1 (page 18)
Single crochet—sc (page 26)
Slip slip knit decrease—ssk (page 19)
Stockinette stitch—St st (page 15)

Size
Small: chest—38″ (96.5cm);
length—22″ (56cm) from back of neck to bottom edge

Medium: chest—40″ (101.5cm);
length—22″ (56cm) from back of neck to bottom edge

Large: chest—42″ (106.5cm); length—22″ (56cm) from back of neck to bottom edge

⊗ ⊗ ⊗

Gauge
13 stitches/20 rows=4″ (10cm)

⊗ ⊗ ⊗

What You'll Need
Yarn: About 952 [952, 1,088] yards (871m [871m, 995m]) 100% wool, heavy worsted weight thick 'n thin yarn **We used:** Manos del Uruguay solids, 100% hand-spun, hand-dyed (100% wool): #68 citric, 7 [7, 8] skeins

Needles: US Size 10½ (6.5 mm)

Notions: 2 long stitch holders; US size J (6.5mm) crochet hook; tapestry needle

Note: Instructions are given for smallest size; all other sizes are in brackets. When only 1 number or set of instructions is given, it applies to all sizes.

Make the cardigan
The cardigan is worked in 1 piece from cuff to cuff. *(See fig. a, page 121.)*
Left sleeve: Cast on 74 stitches at the cuff. Make ruffle as follows:

Row 1: (right side) Knit 2, *purl 6, knit 2**; repeat from * to ** to end of row.

Row 2: (wrong side) Purl 2, *knit 6, purl 2**; repeat from * to ** to end of row.

Row 3: Repeat row 1.

Row 4: (wrong side) Purl 2, *slip slip knit decrease, knit 2, knit 2 together, purl 2**; repeat from * to ** to end of row. (56 stitches)

Row 5: Knit 2, *purl 4, knit 2**; repeat from * to ** to end of row.

Row 6: Purl 2, *slip slip knit decrease, knit 2 together, purl 2**; repeat from * to ** to end of row. (38 stitches)

Row 7: Knit 2, *purl 2, knit 2**; repeat from * to ** to end of row.

Change to stockinette stitch (knit all right-side rows, purl all wrong-side rows). When sleeve measures 10″ (25.5cm) from cast-on edge, begin increases to widen the sleeve to fit upper arm. Beginning with a right-side row, increase 1 stitch (using the make 1 increase method) at each end of every 8th row 5 times (48 stitches). Work even without further increases until sleeve measures 20½″ (65cm) or desired length to armhole.

Cast on stitches for body: As loosely as possible, cast on 44 stitches at the end of each of the next 2 rows (136 stitches including body stitches) using either simple cast-on or cable cast-on method. If you'd like a longer cardigan, simply cast on more stitches here (but remember that you'll need more yarn). Add 3 stitches for approximately every 1 inch of length you wish to add.

Work even in stockinette stitch until piece measures 6″ [6½″, 7″] (15cm [16.5cm, 18cm]) from body cast-on edge.

Make back

Next right-side row: Knit 68 stitches; place remaining 68 stitches on stitch holder. (This is the beginning of the neck opening, and the 68 stitches placed on the holder are for the left front.)

Work even until neck opening measures 7″ (18cm). Back will measure 13″ [13½″, 14″] (33cm [34.5cm, 35.5cm]) from body cast-on edge. Place these 68 stitches on another stitch holder.

Left front: Move the 68 stitches of left front from the holder to needle, and work even in stockinette stitch until piece measures 3½″ (9cm) from edge of neck opening. Bind off these 68 stitches as loosely as possible.

Right front: Cast on 68 stitches as loosely as possible. Work even in stockinette stitch until piece measures 3½″ (9cm) from cast-on edge.

Next wrong-side row: Purl to end of row; slip the 68 stitches of the back onto the empty needle, and purl them onto the same needle as the right front 68 stitches. (You've worked the front and back stitches onto 1 needle).

Work even in stockinette stitch across all 136 stitches, joining the back and the right front at the shoulder. Work even until piece measures 6″ [6½″, 7″] (15cm [16.5cm, 18cm]) from closest neck edge. Bind off 44 stitches as loosely as possible at the beginning of each of the next 2 rows (48 stitches).

Right sleeve: At this point, check the first sleeve (left sleeve) and measure the distance in inches from the edge of the body to the last sleeve increase, which should be about 2½″ (6.5cm). Work even until the right sleeve is that length, and then begin decreasing. Beginning with the next right-side row, decrease 1 stitch (knit 2 together) at each end of every 8th row 5 times (38 stitches). When all decreases are finished, work even in stockinette stitch on 38 stitches until sleeve measures 18¾″ (47.5cm) from bound-off edge

of body stitches. Begin ruffle at sleeve edge with a right-side row as follows:

Row 1: (right side) Knit 2, *purl 2, knit 2**; repeat from * to ** to end of row.

Row 2: (wrong side) Purl 2, *make 1 increase, knit 2, make 1 increase, purl 2*; repeat from * to ** to end of row. (56 stitches)

Row 3: Knit 2, *purl 4, knit 2**; repeat from * to ** to end of row.

Row 4: Purl 2, *make 1, knit 4, make 1, purl 2**; repeat from * to ** to end of row. (74 stitches)

Row 5: Knit 2, *purl 6, knit 2**; repeat from * to ** to end of row.

Row 6: Purl 2, *knit 6, purl 2**; repeat from * to ** to end of row.

Row 7: Knit 2, *purl 6, knit 2**; repeat from * to ** to end of row.

Finishing

Bind off all stitches as loosely as possible. Using backstitch, sew side seams together, leaving the lower 3″ (7.5cm) of each side open for side vents. Continue using backstitch to sew sleeve seams together.

Crochet edge: On vertical edges of knitting, work about 3 single crochet stitches to every 4 knitted rows. On horizontal edges, work about 1 single crochet stitch for every knit stitch. Adjust as necessary if this arrangement doesn't fit your gauge.

With right side facing, and easing the edges as you crochet so as not to stretch or pull knitting, begin at bottom edge of left vent. Single crochet across bottom edge of back of cardigan, along both side edges of right side vent, across bottom edge of right front, along the right center front edge, around neck edge, along left center front, across bottom of left front, along both side edges of left vent, and back to where you began. Join first and last single crochet stitches with a slipstitch as follows: Insert hook into first single crochet made, yarn over hook from back to front, and pull a loop through both loops on hook in

1 motion. Cut yarn, leaving 4″ (10cm) tail, and insert through remaining loop to tighten and secure. Thread tail on tapestry needle and weave through stitches on wrong side of work.

Scallops: Work scallops along both front edges and around neck opening as follows: With right side of work facing, single crochet into the first single crochet at bottom of right front edge, *skip 3 single crochet stitches, work a double crochet 7 times in the next single crochet, skip 3 single crochet stitches, single crochet in next single crochet**; repeat from * to **. Make sure both fronts have the same number of scallops; adjust stitches if necessary. Cut yarn, leaving 4″ (10cm) tail, and insert through remaining loop to tighten and secure. Thread tail on tapestry needle and weave through stitches on wrong side of work. Weave in any remaining loose ends, then block cardigan to measurements *(fig. b)*.

Fig. a

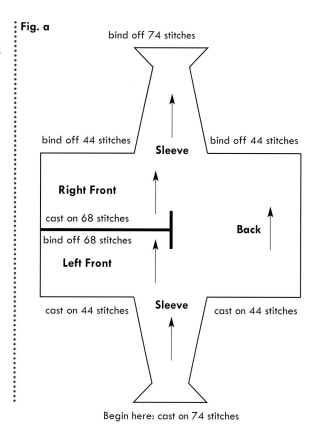

bind off 74 stitches

bind off 44 stitches | bind off 44 stitches

Sleeve

Right Front

cast on 68 stitches

bind off 68 stitches

Back

Left Front

cast on 44 stitches | cast on 44 stitches

Sleeve

Begin here: cast on 74 stitches

Fig. b

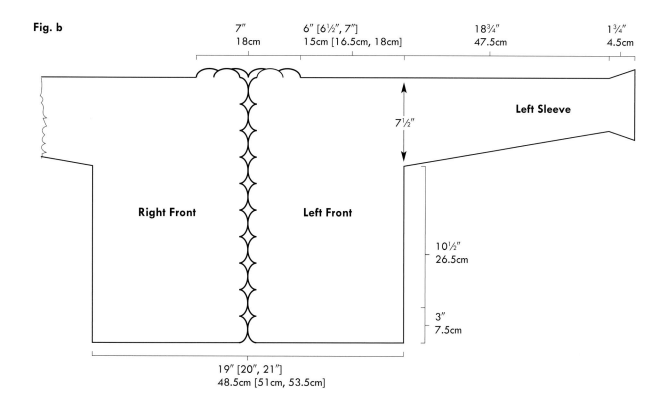

7″ / 18cm   6″ [6½″, 7″] / 15cm [16.5cm, 18cm]   18¾″ / 47.5cm   1¾″ / 4.5cm

Left Sleeve

7½″

Right Front   **Left Front**

10½″ / 26.5cm

3″ / 7.5cm

19″ [20″, 21″] / 48.5cm [51cm, 53.5cm]

Men's Sporty Vest

Great for tennis, golf, or simply wearing around the house on weekends,
this textured vest is knit in one piece and is nicely accented with two contrasting colors.
Wool yarn makes it warm as well as stylish.

Designer: Marilyn King

Techniques

Binding off—BO (page 14)
Blocking (page 27)
Buttonholes (page 21)
Casting on—CO (page 9)
Knit 2 together—k2tog (page 19)
Ribbing (page 15)
Three-needle bind-off (page 24)
Yarn over—yo (page 17)

Sizes

Small: Chest—39″ (99cm)
Medium: Chest—42″ (106.5cm)
Large: Chest—45″ (114.5cm)

❀ ❀ ❀

Gauge

20 stitches/30 rows=4″ (10cm) in
pattern, using size 6 (4mm) needles

❀ ❀ ❀

What You'll Need

Yarn: 100% worsted weight wool yarn:
880 [880, 880] yards (805m [805m,
805m]) color A; 55 yards (50m)
each colors B and C
We used: Black Water Abbey Worsted
Weight (100% wool): Silver (color A),
4 [4, 4] skeins; Forest (color B), 1oz;
Ocean (color C), 1oz

Needles: US size 6 (4mm), 24″ (61cm)
circular; US size 4 (3.5mm)
16″ (40.5cm) circular and 24″ (61cm)
or 29″ (73.5cm) circular

Notions: 2 stitch markers; 7 stitch
holders or scrap yarn; 6 buttons, about
⅝″–¾″ (1.5cm–2cm) in diameter;
6 safety pins; tapestry needle; sewing
needle and matching thread

Note:
• Instructions are given for smallest size. Larger sizes are in brackets. When only
1 number is given, it applies to all sizes.
• Working flat, the vest is made in 1 piece up to the armholes, where it sepa-
rates into 3 sections: right front, left front, and back.

Make the vest

Using size 6 needles and color A, cast on 191 [205, 221] stitches. Place a
stitch marker after 48 [51, 55] stitches and another one after 143 [154,
166] stitches. These mark the center of the armhole, indicating the
2 front pieces and the back.

Begin ribbing: Work in knit 1, purl 1 ribbing for 2″ (5cm). End with
wrong-side row.

Make the body

Row 1: (right side) Knit.
Row 2: (wrong side) Knit 1, purl 1 across row.

Repeat these 2 rows for pattern stitch until work measures 13″ [13½″, 13½″]
(33cm [34.5cm, 34.5cm]) or desired length to armhole. End with wrong-
side row. Cut yarn, leaving 6″ (15cm) tail to weave in later. Place first
42 [45, 49] stitches (right front) on stitch holder. Place next 12 stitches
(underarm) on another stitch holder. Knit across back to within 6 stitches
of stitch marker. Place next 12 stitches on another stitch holder. Place
remaining 42 [45, 49] stitches (left front) on another stitch holder.

Make the back: Begin armhole shaping. Continue pattern, decreasing
1 stitch at each armhole edge, every other row, 8 [9, 9] times. Work even
in pattern on remaining 67 [73, 81] stitches until armhole measures
9″ [9½″, 9½″] (23cm [24cm, 24cm]). Place stitches on stitch holders as
follows: 20 [22, 25] stitches on first holder (shoulder stitches), 27 [29, 31]
stitches on next holder (back neckline), 20 [22, 25] stitches on last stitch
holder (shoulder stitches).

Make the front panels: Knit the 2 fronts simultaneously. Attach another
ball of yarn to outside edge of right front. Knit in pattern to end of row,
decrease 1 stitch. Attach another ball of yarn to underarm side of left

front, decrease 1 stitch, knit in pattern to end of row. Continue to decrease 1 stitch every other row on armhole side 7 [8, 8] more times (34 [36, 40] stitches remain). When armhole decreases are finished, begin neckline shaping: Decrease 1 stitch at inside edge of each front panel. Continue to decrease 1 stitch every third row 13 [13, 14] more times (20 [22, 25] stitches). Work even in pattern until armhole length matches back armhole. Join fronts and back shoulder stitches using three-needle bind-off.

Make the armhole bands: Slip 12 underarm stitches from stitch holder onto smaller 16″ (40.5cm) circular needles. Attach color B, and pick up approximately 88 [98, 98] stitches evenly around armhole (100 [110, 110] stitches). Armhole bands are worked flat, back and forth as follows:

Row 1: (wrong side) With color B, knit 1, purl 1 ribbing to end of row.

Row 2: (right side) With color C, knit.

Row 3: With color C, knit 1, purl 1 ribbing to end of row.

Row 4: With color C, purl 1, knit 1 ribbing to end of row.

Row 5: With color A, purl.

Row 6: With color A, purl 1, knit 1 ribbing to end of row.

Row 7: With color A, knit 1, purl 1 ribbing to end of row.

With color A, bind off in rib pattern. Cut yarn, leaving a 6″ (15cm) tail to weave in later.

Repeat for other armhole.

Begin the front band: With right side facing and using size 4 circular needles, either 24″ (61cm) or 29″ (73.5cm), and color B, pick up approximately 74 [78, 78] stitches along front of vest, then 36 [40, 40] stitches along front neckline. Knit across 27 [29, 31] back neckline stitches, pick up 36 [40, 40] stitches along other front neckline and 74 [78, 78] stitches down the other front edge (247 [265, 267] stitches

total). Knit front band in same 7-row pattern as armhole bands. At the same time, on the third row, make buttonholes on the left-side band.

Make the buttonholes: Before starting buttonhole row, spread front band stitches over 2 circular needles so front edge is flat and smooth. Determine buttonhole spacing by placing first button about 5 stitches up from lower edge and last button just before beginning of front neckline shaping. Mark these 2 spots with safety pins, and arrange remaining buttons in between. Once you've decided where to place the buttons, count the stitches between buttons, and use this number to space the buttonholes. Mark the places on buttonhole side of band with safety pins. You may prefer to use more or fewer buttons than suggested for this pattern. Before you resume pattern, slip front stitches back onto working needle, removing second needle.

Beginning at the lower edge, work the first buttonhole in pattern about 5 stitches from lower edge as follows: yarn over, knit 2 together (first buttonhole). Repeat for each of the remaining buttonholes at the places marked with safety pins. The last buttonhole should be located just before front neckline shaping begins. Continue with ribbing pattern to end of row. Knit remaining 4 rows of ribbing pattern. Bind off in ribbing pattern.

Finishing

Weave in yarn tails to wrong side of work; secure. Block vest to desired size. Place vest on flat surface, and with sewing needle and thread, attach buttons, aligning them with buttonholes.

Straighten Out

Sometimes your circular needles will be curled so tightly that they will be difficult to use. To straighten them, dip them into hot water for up to 30 seconds and then lay flat to dry. Try to store your needles straightened out to full length to reduce the curl so they are ready when you are.

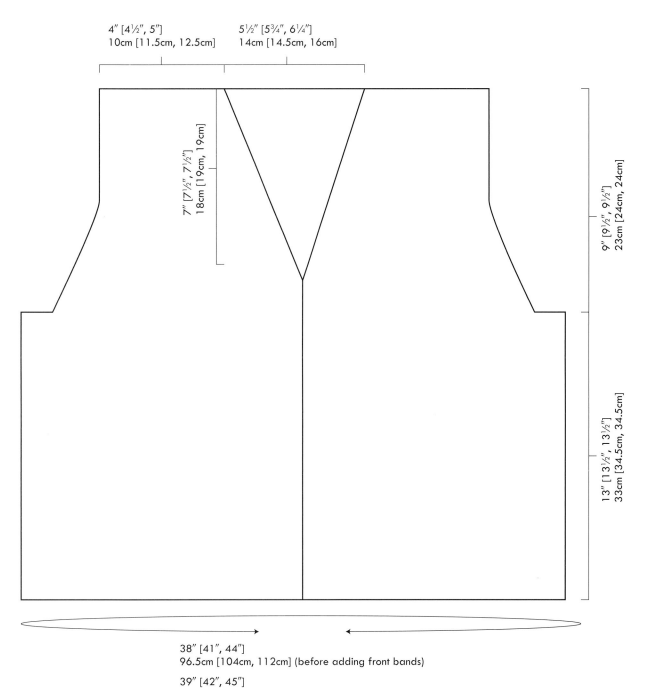

4" [4½", 5"]
10cm [11.5cm, 12.5cm]

5½" [5¾", 6¼"]
14cm [14.5cm, 16cm]

7" [7½", 7½"]
18cm [19cm, 19cm]

9" [9½", 9½"]
23cm [24cm, 24cm]

13" [13½", 13½"]
33cm [34.5cm, 34.5cm]

38" [41", 44"]
96.5cm [104cm, 112cm] (before adding front bands)

39" [42", 45"]
99cm [106.5cm, 114.5cm] (with front bands)

Monet Cardigan

Gorgeous yarn transforms a simple cardigan-style sweater into a work of art. There's a reason this yarn is named after master artist Monet: Its bright, high-keyed hues capture natural light and sparkling color. Truly a masterpiece!

Designer: Berroco, Inc.

Size

Extra small: chest—36" (91.5cm), length—21½" (54.5cm)

Small: chest—40" (101.5cm), length—22" (56cm)

Medium: chest—44" (112cm), length—22½" (57cm)

Large: chest—48" (122cm), length—22½" (57cm)

Extra large: chest—54" (137cm), length—23" (58.5cm)

Gauge

14 stitches/24 rows=4" (10cm) in reverse stockinette stitch

What You'll Need

Yarn: 833 [882, 931, 980, 1029] yards (765m [810m, 855m, 900m, 945m]) designer yarn spun as mixture of boucle and slubs in blend of synthetic fibers and small amount of cotton
We used: Berroco Monet (42% rayon, 36% acrylic, 13% cotton, 9% nylon; 49 yards [45m]/50g): #3393 Water Lilies, 17 [18, 19, 20, 21] skeins

Needles: US size 10 (6mm)

Notions: 5 buttons, 1" (2.5cm) each; sewing needle and thread to match; steam iron; pressing cloth; tapestry needle; few yards smooth yarn in matching color for sewing seams

Note: Instructions are given for smallest size. Larger sizes are in brackets. When only 1 number or set of instructions is given, it applies to all sizes.

Make the back

Cast on 73 [80, 87, 94, 105] stitches. Work even in garter stitch for 1" (2.5cm), then work in reverse stockinette stitch for 2 rows, ending on wrong-side row (this is the smooth knit row in reverse stockinette stitch).

Decrease row: (right side) Purl 1, purl 2 together, purl to last 3 stitches, purl 2 together, purl 1 (71 [78, 85, 92, 103] stitches). Repeat this row every 3½" (9cm) 3 more times (65 [72, 79, 86, 97] stitches), working even in reverse stockinette between decrease rows.

Work even until piece measures 12½" (31.5cm) from cast-on edge, ending with wrong-side row.

Shape the armholes: Bind off 2 stitches at beginning of next 2 rows. (61 [68, 75, 82, 93] stitches)

Decrease row: (right side) Purl 2, purl 2 together, purl to last 4 stitches, purl 2 together, purl 2 (59 [66, 73, 80, 91] stitches). Repeat this row on every right-side row 7 more times (45 [52, 59, 66, 77] stitches), and knit the wrong-side rows.

Techniques

Backstitch (page 23)
Bar increase (page 18)
Increases—inc (page 17)
Purl 2 together—p2tog (page 19)
Reverse stockinette stitch (page 15)
Yarn over—yo (page 17)

Working with Monet Yarn

- When knitting your gauge swatch, keep track of the rows and stitches knit and then measure the gauge over the entire swatch. Due to the nature of the yarn, it's difficult to count stitches and rows after it's knit.

- Keep track of the number of rows worked throughout the project. This ensures that the back and front pieces will be exactly the same length.

- Sew seams using a smooth yarn in a similar color to match the garment.

Work even in reverse stockinette stitch until armholes measure 8″ [8½″, 9″, 9″, 9½″] (20.5cm [21.5cm, 23cm, 23cm, 24cm]), ending with wrong-side row.

Shape the shoulders and neck: Bind off 4 [5, 6, 7, 9] stitches at beginning of next 4 rows. Then bind off 4 [5, 6, 7, 8] stitches at beginning of next 2 rows. Bind off remaining 21 [22, 23, 24, 25] stitches for back neck.

Make the left front

Cast on 39 [42, 46, 50, 54] stitches. Work even in garter stitch for 1″ (2.5cm). Keeping 1 stitch at front edge in garter stitch, work remaining stitches in reverse stockinette stitch for 2 rows. End with wrong-side row.

Decrease row: (right side) Purl 1, purl 2 together, purl to end of row (38 [41, 45, 49, 53] stitches). Repeat this row every 3½″ (9cm) 3 more times (35 [38, 42, 46, 50] stitches), working even in reverse stockinette stitch between decrease rows.

Work even until piece measures 12½″ (31.5cm) from cast-on edge, ending with wrong-side row.

Shape the armhole: (right side) Bind off 2 stitches at beginning of row, purl to last stitch, knit 1 (33 [36, 40, 44, 48] stitches). Knit 1 row.

Next row: (right side) Purl 2, purl 2 together, purl to last stitch, knit 1 (32 [35, 39, 43, 47] stitches). Repeat this row on every right-side row 7 more times (25 [28, 32, 36, 40] stitches), and knit the wrong-side rows.

Work even in reverse stockinette stitch until armhole measures 6½″ [7″, 7½″, 7½″, 8″] (16.5cm [18cm, 19cm, 19cm, 20.5cm]), ending with right-side row.

Shape the neck: (wrong side) Bind off 4 [4, 5, 6, 5] stitches, knit to end (21 [24, 27, 30, 35] stitches).

Next row: (right side) Purl 1 row. Beginning at neck edge, *on wrong-side rows only,* bind off 4 stitches once, then bind off 3 stitches once, then purl 2 together at neck edge every *right-side* row 2 times (12 [15, 18, 21, 26] stitches).

When armhole measures 8″ [8½″, 9″, 9″, 9½″] (20.5cm [21.5cm, 23cm, 23cm, 24cm]), end with wrong-side row. Bind off 4 [5, 6, 7, 9] stitches at armhole edge 2 times, then remaining 4 [5, 6, 7, 8] stitches 1 time for shoulder.

Make the right front

Work same as for left front until piece measures 2″ (5cm) from cast-on edge, ending with wrong-side row.

Form buttonhole row: (right side) Knit 1, purl 2, yarn over, purl 2 together, purl to end of row.

Complete right front to correspond with left front, reversing all shaping and making 4 more buttonholes along front edge, spaced 4″ (10cm) apart.

Make the sleeves

Cast on 31 [31, 34, 34, 36] stitches. Work in garter stitch for 1″ (2.5cm), then work even in reverse stockinette stitch for 2 rows, ending with wrong-side row.

Next row: (right side) Purl 1, purl into front and back loop of next stitch (1 increase made), purl to last 2 stitches, purl into front and back loop of next stitch (1 increase made), purl 1 (33 [33, 36, 36, 38] stitches).

Stretching Your Knitting Muscles

Knitting for long periods of time may leave you feeling stiff and sore—don't let it! Sit in a comfortable chair with plenty of back support. Prop pillows under your elbows for support, and knit on circular needles to help distribute the weight of your knitting.

For pain caused by carpal tunnel syndrome, buy a wrist brace or wrap a flexible bandage or gel-filled eye mask around your wrist. Arthritis sufferers, experiment with different ways of holding the needles and yarn to find the most comfortable method.

Take frequent breaks! Plan to stop at the end of certain sections: Work to the end of a row, make a note in the pattern where you stopped, and get up and walk around, stretching your muscles as you go.

Repeat this row every 8th row 0 [1, 6, 6, 11] more times, then every 10th row 5 [9, 5, 5, 1] times, then every 12th row 4 [0, 0, 0, 0] times (51 [53, 58, 58, 62] stitches). Work even until sleeve measures 17½" (44.5cm) from cast-on edge. End with wrong-side row.

Shape cap: Bind off 2 stitches at beginning of next 2 rows (47 [49, 54, 54, 58] stitches). Work 2 rows even in reverse stockinette stitch.

Next row: (right side) Purl 2, purl 2 together, purl to last 4 stitches, purl 2 together, purl 2 (45 [47, 52, 52, 56] stitches). Repeat this row every other right-side row (every 4th row) 3 more times, ending on wrong-side row (39 [41, 46, 46, 50] stitches). Bind off all stitches.

Repeat all steps for second sleeve.

Finishing

Block pieces with steam iron and pressing cloth. Allow to air-dry. With smooth yarn in matching color threaded on tapestry needle, and using backstitch for all seams, sew shoulder seams. Sew in sleeves. Sew side and sleeve seams. With matching sewing thread and needle, sew on buttons.

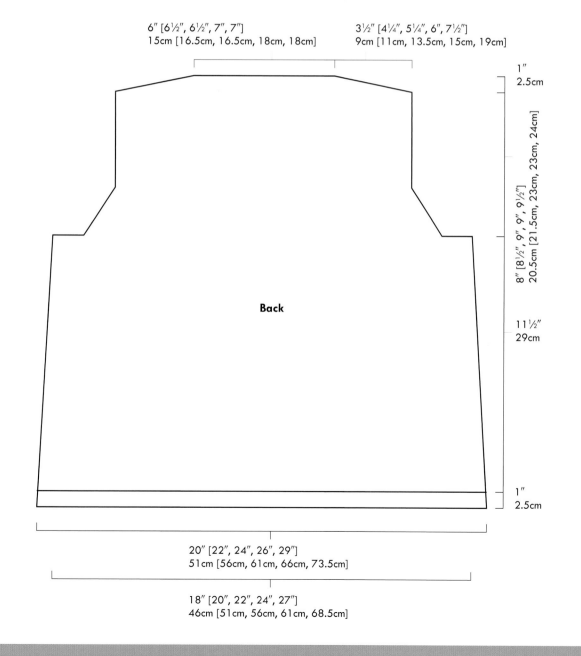

6" [6½", 6½", 7", 7"]
15cm [16.5cm, 16.5cm, 18cm, 18cm]

3½" [4¼", 5¼", 6", 7½"]
9cm [11cm, 13.5cm, 15cm, 19cm]

1"
2.5cm

8" [8½", 9", 9", 9½"]
20.5cm [21.5cm, 23cm, 23cm, 24cm]

Back

11½"
29cm

1"
2.5cm

20" [22", 24", 26", 29"]
51cm [56cm, 61cm, 66cm, 73.5cm]

18" [20", 22", 24", 27"]
46cm [51cm, 56cm, 61cm, 68.5cm]

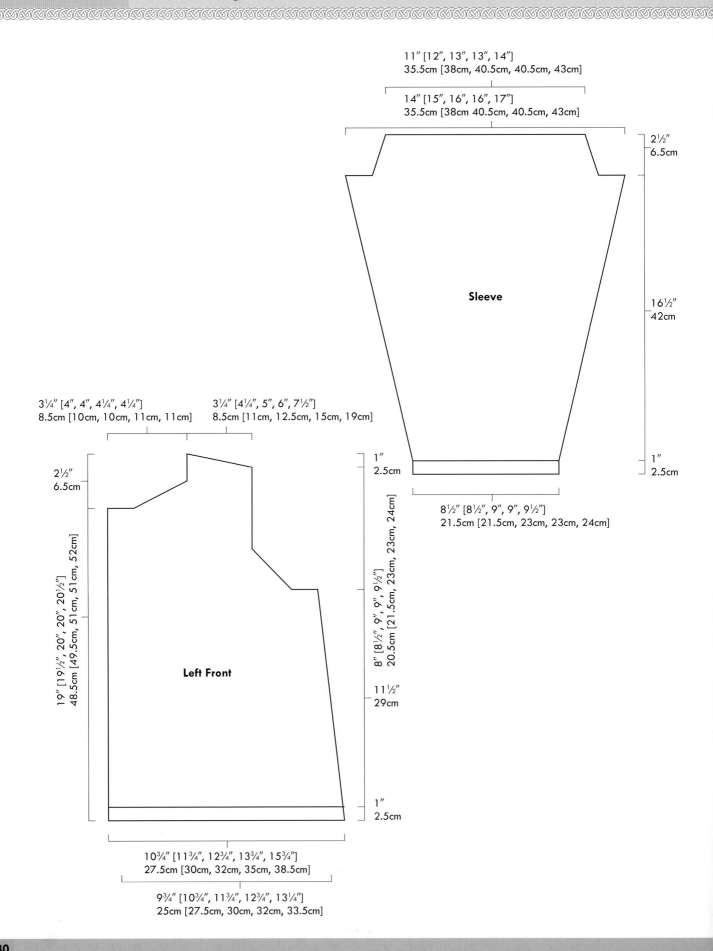

11" [12", 13", 13", 14"]
35.5cm [38cm, 40.5cm, 40.5cm, 43cm]

14" [15", 16", 16", 17"]
35.5cm [38cm 40.5cm, 40.5cm, 43cm]

2½"
6.5cm

Sleeve

16½"
42cm

1"
2.5cm

8½" [8½", 9", 9", 9½"]
21.5cm [21.5cm, 23cm, 23cm, 24cm]

3¼" [4", 4", 4¼", 4¼"]
8.5cm [10cm, 10cm, 11cm, 11cm]

3¼" [4¼", 5", 6", 7½"]
8.5cm [11cm, 12.5cm, 15cm, 19cm]

2½"
6.5cm

1"
2.5cm

19" [19½", 20", 20", 20½"]
48.5cm [49.5cm, 51cm, 51cm, 52cm]

8" [8½", 9", 9", 9½"]
20.5cm [21.5cm, 23cm, 23cm, 24cm]

11½"
29cm

Left Front

1"
2.5cm

10¾" [11¾", 12¾", 13¾", 15¾"]
27.5cm [30cm, 32cm, 35cm, 38.5cm]

9¾" [10¾", 11¾", 12¾", 13¼"]
25cm [27.5cm, 30cm, 32cm, 33.5cm]

Winter Warmth

When it's cold and snowy outside, turn to the pleasure of a handmade hat, a beautiful scarf, or fuzzy, fluffy mittens to keep you warm and toasty. And don't slippers and socks you've made yourself feel all the more cozy because of it?

Simple Sparkle Scarf

Knit in simple garter stitch, this easy-to-make scarf can be completed in just a couple of evenings. The sparkly yarn is irresistible in all colors. You'll be amazed at how many different looks you can achieve just by changing the yarn. Don't be afraid to experiment!　Designer: Lucie Sinkler

Size

7×52″ (18×132cm)

⊛　⊛　⊛

Gauge

12 stitches=4″ (10cm) in garter stitch.
Exact gauge is not important; scarf can be slightly wider or narrower

⊛　⊛　⊛

What You'll Need

Yarn: 180 yards (165m) medium weight mohair blend yarn with glitz; or use 2 yarns held together as 1, 180 yards (165m) mohair blend and 180 yards (16m) glitzy thread or thin yarn
We used: Trendsetter Yarns Dune: red #91, 2 balls (red scarf); blue #39, 2 balls (blue scarf); green #93, 2 balls (green scarf)

Needles: US size 11 (8mm)

Notion: Tapestry needle

Make the scarf

Cast on 20 stitches, leaving 4″ (10cm) tail. Work in garter stitch (knit every row) until scarf measures about 52″ (132cm), or keep knitting until just enough yarn remains to bind off all stitches and secure yarn tail (about 4 times the scarf width plus 6″ [15cm]).

Bind off all stitches loosely; try to match the same elasticity as the cast-on edge. Cut yarn, leaving 4″ (10cm) tail. Thread tapestry needle and weave through bound-off stitches to secure. Weave in yarn tail at cast-on edge in same manner.

 Tip

Techniques

Binding off—BO (page 14)
Casting on—CO (page 9)
Garter stitch (page 15)
Knit stitch–k (page 12)
Weaving in yarn tails (page 25)

Take Good Care of Your Yarn

There may come a time when temptation has won and you've collected far more yarn than you can knit in the near future. You must store it properly so it will be ready when you are. Sunlight, mildew, and moths are the three major enemies of yarn. Store extra yarn away from direct sunlight so it won't fade. Avoid mildew by making sure the yarn is completely dry before you store it and by allowing enough air to circulate in the storage box. Use a cardboard box with a loose-fitting lid or a plastic storage box with the lid partially off (or you can drill a few holes in the box). To discourage the third enemy, moths, cedar blocks or sachets are a nicer-smelling option than mothballs.

Double-Knit Slippers

This simple slipper is a breeze to knit and is extra-cushy because it is worked in double knit. This design is perfect for a man, woman, or child—just choose your yarn accordingly—and even a beginner could whip up a pair in just a weekend.

Designer: Laurie Gonyea

Techniques

Binding off–BO (page 14)
Casting on–CO (page 9)
Mattress stitch (page 23)
Ribbing (page 15)
Slipping stitches purlwise (page 16)

Sizes

Small: 7″ (18cm) in length
Medium: 9″ (23cm) in length
Large: 10″ (25.5cm) in length

⊛   ⊛   ⊛

Gauge

24 stitches/32 rows=4″ (10cm)
in double-knit pattern stitch

⊛   ⊛   ⊛

What You'll Need

Yarn: About 76 (124) yards 100% wool
We used: Kiparoo Farm Featherlite Bulky: Large slippers—natural silver-gray, 2 skeins; medium slippers—coral, 2 skeins; small slippers—turquoise, 1 skein

Needles: US size 8 (5mm)

Notions: Tapestry needle; 2 buttons, each ¾″ (2cm) in diameter (*optional*); sewing needle and thread to match

Notes:

• Instructions are given for smallest size; larger sizes are in brackets.
• To make sure the slippers fit snugly and stay on the wearer's feet, you may need to adjust the size. Each 8 rows worked in the row gauge will make 1″ (2.5cm) in length. To make shorter slippers, knit fewer rows; for longer slippers, knit more rows. If you want the cuffs to reach farther up from the ankle toward the calf, simply work a few more inches in ribbing until the desired height is achieved.

Double-knit Pattern Stitch
Row 1: (right side) [Knit 1, purl 1]; repeat across row, ending with knit 1.
Row 2: (wrong side) [Knit 1, slip 1 stitch purlwise]; repeat across row, ending with knit 1.

Make the slippers

Cast on 31 [37, 37] stitches, leaving a 12″ (30.5cm) tail to use later when sewing back heel seam. Work in double-knit pattern stitch until work measures 5″ [7″, 7″] (12.5cm [18cm, 18cm]) from cast-on edge. End with right-side row.

Make the toe

The wrong side of the stitch pattern becomes the right side; the right side of the pattern becomes the wrong side.
Row 1: (wrong side) Work row 1 of double-knit pattern stitch.
Row 2: (right side) Work row 2 of double-knit pattern stitch.
Repeat rows 1 and 2 until entire piece measures 6½″ [8½″, 9½″] (16.5cm [21.5cm, 24cm]) from cast-on edge. End with wrong-side row.

Shape the toe

Row 1: (right side) Knit 1, [knit 2 together, slip 1 purlwise, knit 1]; repeat instructions in brackets to end of row, ending child's size with slip 1, knit 1. (24[28, 28] stitches)
Row 2: (wrong side) Purl.
Row 3: [Knit 1, knit 2 together]; repeat to end of row, ending adult sizes with knit 1. (16 [19, 19] stitches)
Row 4: Purl.
Row 5 (size small only): Knit 2 together; repeat to end of row. (8 stitches)

Slip Tip

Knit slippers are slippery on uncarpeted floors and stairs. It's a good idea to add leather nonslip slipper soles or use puff paints across the underfoot section of the slipper. Both items are available at craft stores.

Row 5 (medium and large only): Knit 1, [knit 2 together] to end of row. (10 stitches)

Finishing body of slipper

Cut yarn, leaving 24″ (61cm) tail. Thread yarn tail on tapestry needle, and insert through remaining 8 [10, 10] stitches. Pull yarn firmly, closing toe stitches together. With right side facing, use the same yarn and needle to sew a 5″ (12.5cm) seam from toe along top of slipper (use mattress stitch for ribbing section, and backstitch the garter stitch edges together). Weave yarn tails to wrong side of work, and secure yarn by weaving through several stitches. Fold slipper in half, lengthwise, and sew the 2 heel edges together to close slipper.

Make the cuff: Pick up 1 stitch at end of every garter stitch ridge row around the ankle (make sure you end with an even number). Work back and forth in knit 1, purl 1 ribbing for 1½″ (3.8cm) or desired length. Cut yarn, leaving 4″ (10cm) tail. Weave loose ends to wrong side, and secure.

Repeat all steps for matching slipper.

Optional: With sewing thread and needle, attach a decorative button to instep of each slipper as shown in photo.

Wavy Rib Socks

Warm, comfy socks are fun to make and great to wear, and our Wavy Rib Socks are no exception. Once you've knit one pair, you may want to make a pair in every color. They look terrific in teal…just imagine all the other colorful possibilities.

Designer: Charlene Hatfield

Techniques

Binding off—BO (page 14)

Casting on—CO (page 9)

Kitchener stitch (page 24)

Knit 2 stitches together—k2tog
(page 19)

Knitting with double-pointed needles
(page 16)

Purl 2 stitches together—p2tog
(page 19)

Slipping stitches knitwise, purlwise
(page 16)

Slip slip knit decrease—ssk (page 19)

Weaving in yarn tails (page 25)

Working with double-pointed
needles—dpn (page 16)

Size

Adult: leg length, 6½" (16.5cm) to
beginning of heel flap; foot length,
9" (23cm)
*Leg and foot length can be adjusted
to fit wearer.*

⊗ ⊗ ⊗

Gauge

24 stitches/34 rows=4" (10cm)
in stockinette stitch on size
2 (2.75mm) needles

⊗ ⊗ ⊗

What You'll Need

Yarn: 378–400 yards (346–366m)
sportweight mohair and wool blend yarn
We used: Dale of Norway Tiur (60%
mohair, 40% wool) #7053, 3 balls (if
making larger socks, buy 1 extra ball)

Needles: US size 4 (3.5mm) double-
pointed needles, set of 5; US size
2 (2.75mm) double-pointed, set of 5

Notions: Stitch marker;
tapestry needle

Make the socks

With size 4 double-pointed needles, cast on 60 stitches and join into a circle, being careful not to twist stitches. Transfer stitches to size 2 needles, working 1 needle at a time and slipping stitches purlwise. Divide the stitches equally, with 15 on each needle. Attach stitch marker to first stitch so it won't slip off end of needle, then move it up to the current round every few rounds.

The first needle (holding marker) is needle #1, the next needle (going clockwise) is #2, the next is #3, and the last is #4. Needles #2 and #3 hold the 30 instep stitches during heel shaping.

Leg

Work Wavy Rib pattern as follows:

Rounds 1–4: Purl 2, knit 4; repeat to end of round.
Rounds 5–8: Knit 3, purl 2, [knit 4, purl 2]; repeat instructions in brackets to last stitch; knit 1.

Work 8 complete pattern repeats or until leg measures 7" (18cm) from cast-on edge, ending with round 8.

Begin heel flap Work 15 stitches in pattern. Turn work to wrong side, purl back across the same 15 stitches. Slip marker, then purl across 15 stitches from needle #4. Work flap back and forth in heel stitch (as follows) on the same 30 stitches:

Row 1: (right side) [Slip 1, knit 1]; repeat to end of row, turn work.
Row 2: (wrong side) Slip 1, purl 29 stitches to end of row, turn work.

Repeat these 2 rows for a total of 25 rows or desired length, ending with row 1.

Begin heel turn The heel turn is shaped using short rows, which means that some stitches will not be worked each row, but will remain on the needle. Follow instructions carefully.

Row 1: Slip 1, purl 16, purl 2 together, purl 1; turn work, leaving remaining stitches on needle.
Row 2: Slip 1, knit 5, slip slip knit decrease, knit 1, turn work.
Row 3: Slip 1, purl 6, purl 2 together, purl 1, turn work.
Row 4: Slip 1, knit 7, slip slip knit decrease, knit 1, turn work.
Row 5: Slip 1, purl 8, purl 2 together, purl 1, turn work.
Row 6: Slip 1, knit 9, slip slip knit decrease, knit 1, turn work.
Row 7: Slip 1, purl 10, purl 2 together, purl 1, turn work.

Row 8: Slip 1, knit 11, slip slip knit decrease, knit 1, turn work.

Row 9: Slip 1, purl 12, purl 2 together, purl 1, turn work.

Row 10: Slip 1, knit 13, slip slip knit decrease, knit 1, turn work.

Row 11: Slip 1, purl 14, purl 2 together, purl 1, turn work.

Row 12: Slip 1, knit 15, slip slip knit decrease, knit 1. (18 stitches remain)

Make heel gusset: Continuing with the same needle (holding the 18 heel stitches), pick up and knit 15 stitches along the side edge of the heel flap side; work row 1 of Wavy Rib pattern across the next 30 stitches (needles #2 and #3). With empty needle, pick up and knit 15 stitches along the other side of the heel flap, and knit 9 heel stitches from first needle. Keep stitch marker in place to indicate beginning of rounds. Needle #1 has 24 knit stitches, needle #2 has 15 stitches worked in Wavy Rib pattern, needle #3 has 15 stitches worked in Wavy Rib pattern, and needle #4 has 24 knit stitches (78 stitches total).

Continue rounds:

Round 1: Needle #1–knit; needle #2–work Wavy Rib pattern as established; needle #3–work Wavy Rib pattern as established; needle #4–knit.

Round 2: Needle #1–knit to last 3 stitches, knit 2 together, knit 1; needle #2–work in established pattern; needle #3–work in established pattern; needle #4–knit 1, slip slip knit decrease, knit to end of round.

Work the above 2 rounds until 60 stitches remain (18 rounds).

Make foot: Work in established patterns without further decreases until foot measures about 2″ (5cm) from desired length.

Toe shaping: Working in circular stockinette stitch, knit all rounds as follows:

Round 1: Needle #1–knit to last 3 stitches, knit 2 together, knit 1; needle #2–knit 1, slip slip knit decrease, knit to end of needle; needle #3–knit to last 3 stitches, knit 2 together, knit 1; needle #4–knit 1, slip slip knit decrease, knit to end of round.

Round 2: Knit.

Repeat rounds 1 and 2 until 20 stitches remain. (5 stitches on each needle)

Needles #1 and #4 hold the lower sock stitches, needles #2 and #3 hold the upper sock stitches. Knit to end of needle #1. Slip 5 stitches from needle #4 onto needle #1, then slip stitches from needle #3 onto needle #2. (10 stitches on both needles)

Cut yarn, leaving about 18″ (46 cm) tail. Thread tapestry needle, and weave toe stitches together with Kitchener stitch. Weave in all loose ends to wrong side of work, and secure.

Repeat all steps for second sock.

Hand-wash and block socks before wearing.

Now You See It

Who wouldn't want to knit faster and make fewer mistakes? Try this:

- Make a photocopy of your pattern, and circle or highlight all the numbers for the size you are making. This way, you'll be able to see them at a glance as you work.

- Purchase a vinyl page protector from an office supply store, and put your pattern inside. Use a dry-erase pen to make notes. (The shiny page protectors will erase more easily than those with a matte finish.) Be careful about where you store your marked pages—the dry-erase ink could rub off on your yarn.

"It's a Cinch" Hat

This children's hat is a great project for learning how to knit in the round. The body of the hat is worked straight up without shaping and is then "cinched" at the top with playful twisted cords. The flowers are embroidered using duplicate stitch.

Designer: Beth Walker O'Brien

Techniques

Binding off—BO (page 14)

Casting on—CO (page 9)

Duplicate stitch (page 25)

Knitting in the round (page 16)

Long tail cast-on (page 10)

Ribbing (page 15)

Working with double-pointed needles—dpn (page 16)

Sizes

2–4 years: 16" (40.5cm) in circumference, 7" (18cm) in height

6–8 years: 17" (43cm) in circumference, 7¼" (18.5cm) in height

10–12 years: 18" (46cm) in circumference, 7½" (19cm) in height

❀ ❀ ❀

Gauge

24 stitches/36 rounds=4" (10cm) in circular stockinette stitch

❀ ❀ ❀

What You'll Need

Yarn: Soft, synthetic DK weight yarn: 183 yards (168m)/50g) each color

We used: Plymouth Dreambaby: #112 purple (color A), 1 ball; #116 pink (color B), 1 ball; #114 orange (color C), 1 ball

Needles: US size 5 (3.75mm) circular, 16" (40.5cm) long; US size 7 (4.5mm) circular, 16" (40.5cm) long; US size 7 (4.5mm) set of 5 double-pointed

Notions: Stitch marker; tapestry needle

Note: Instructions are given for the smallest size; larger sizes are in brackets.

Make the hat

With size 5 circular needles and color A, cast on 96 [102, 108] stitches. Join stitches into a circle, taking care not to twist the stitches.

Begin ribbing pattern: Place stitch marker to indicate beginning of round, and work 1 round of knit 1, purl 1 ribbing. Maintain ribbing pattern for next 12 rounds, working as follows: *Change to color B and work 2 rounds. Change to color C and work 2 rounds. Change to color A and work 2 rounds**. Repeat from * to **.

Make the hat body: Using size 7 circular needles and color A, begin circular stockinette stitch, knitting every row until stockinette portion of work measures 7" [7¼", 7½"] (18cm [18.5cm, 19cm]). Change to double-pointed needles by slipping stitches from circular needle onto 4 double-pointed needles, dividing stitches onto needles as follows: 24 stitches on each needle for smallest size hat, 25/26/25/26 stitches for next size, and 27 stitches on each needle for largest size hat.

Knit 2 together around entire hat (48 [51, 54] stitches). Cut yarn, leaving 24" (61cm) tail. Thread tail on tapestry needle, and slip remaining stitches onto yarn tail.

Make the flowers: Use color chart (below) to duplicate-stitch 5 flowers spaced evenly around front of hat, centered between the beginning and end of the stockinette stitch portion and spaced 6 knit stitches apart. Alternate the flower colors so 3 flowers have petals in color B with a color C center and 2 flowers have petals in color C with a color B center.

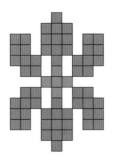 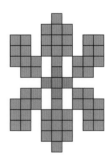

Make the cords: Cut one 4½″ (11.5cm) length of color A; set aside. Cut seven 28″ (71cm) lengths each of color A, B, and C (21 strands total). Keeping the 7 strands of each color together, tie an overhand knot at each end. Holding the group of yarns with 1 hand at each end, insert a knitting needle through 1 end and begin twisting while holding the other end still. Continue twisting until the yarns entwine neatly upon themselves when doubled in half. Using the 4½″ (11.5cm) length of color A, knot 1 strand of yarn about 4½″ (11.5cm) from the fold to secure twist. Untie original overhand knots. Repeat 2 more times for a total of 3 tassels. Trim the free ends of the tassels to 1½″ (3.8cm) from the tie.

Finishing

Thread yarn tail at top of hat through the folds of each twisted cord; pull top tightly closed. Insert needle and yarn tail to wrong side of hat, and weave in ends. Weave in all remaining ends.

Fun Felted Mittens

Slip your hands into these soft woolen mittens for a real winter warm-up! Perfect as a gift or to add to your own collection of winter gear, this pretty pair is first knit and then shrunk in the washing machine to achieve a felted look.

Designer: Lucie Sinkler

Techniques

Binding off—BO (page 14)

Casting on—CO (page 9)

Felting (page 27)

Knitting in the round (page 16)

Make 1 increase—m1 (page 18)

Picking up stitches (page 22)

Simple cast-on (page 11)

Slipping stitches knitwise,
purlwise (page 16)

Working with 2 yarns as 1 (page 21)

Working with double-pointed
needles—dpn (page 16)

Size

Adult medium: 9″ (23cm) in length,
8″ (20.5cm) in circumference
measured around palm
(after felting)

❀　❀　❀

Gauge

18 stitches=4″ (10cm)

❀　❀　❀

What You'll Need

Yarn: 220 yards (201m) medium
weight 100% wool yarn;
50g fuzzy yarn
*(Superwash wool and synthetics will not
felt; do not use for felting projects.)*
We used: Cascade Yarns Cascade
(100% wool): #220 (yarn A), 1 skein;
Schachenmayr Salsa (100% polyester):
#49 dark purple (yarn B), 1 ball

Needles: US size 8 (5mm) set of
5 double-pointed

Notions: Stitch markers; tapestry
needle; small amount of waste yarn to
use as stitch holder

Miscellaneous: Washing machine,
dishwashing liquid

Make the mittens

Holding both yarns together as 1, cast on 44 stitches. Divide stitches equally onto 4 needles (11 stitches on each needle). Join stitches into a circle, taking care not to twist stitches. Place stitch marker at beginning of round. Knit in circular stockinette stitch (knit all rounds) until work measures 3½″ (9cm) from cast-on edge. Cut yarn B, leaving 5″ (12.5cm) tail. Weave tail to wrong side of work, and secure.

Continue with yarn A as follows:

Round 1: [Knit 5, make 1] 8 times; knit 4. (52 stitches)

Rounds 2–11: Knit.

Begin thumb gusset: (Use the same color markers to indicate beginning and end of increases, but choose a different color than beginning-of-round marker.)

Round 12: Knit 2, place stitch marker to indicate beginning of increases, make 1, knit 2, make 1. Place stitch marker to indicate end of increases, knit to end of round. (54 stitches)

Round 13: Knit.

Round 14: Knit to first increase marker, slip marker, make 1, knit to next increase marker, make 1, slip marker, knit to end of round. (56 stitches)

Repeat rounds 13 and 14 five more times until there are 16 stitches between increase markers and 66 stitches total on needles.

Round 25: Knit.

Round 26: Knit to first marker. Thread piece of waste yarn on tapestry needle. Slip the 16 stitches between increase markers onto waste yarn; tie yarn ends together to hold stitches. With yarn A and the same needle used to begin the round, cast on 2 stitches using the simple cast-on method (these will become 2 new stitches in the next round). Knit to end of round. (52 stitches on needle, including cast-on stitches)

Continue knitting in rounds until work measures 11″ (28cm) from cuff.

Shape top of mitten

Round 1: [Knit 2, knit 2 together] 13 times. (39 stitches)

Rounds 2–5: Knit.

Round 6: [Knit 1, knit 2 together] 13 times. (26 stitches)

Rounds 7–10: Knit.

Round 11: [Knit 2 together] 13 times. (13 stitches)

Round 12: Knit.

Cut yarn, leaving 5″ (12.5cm) tail. Thread tapestry needle, and insert through 13 stitches on needles. Pull yarn gently to close mitten top. Turn inside out, and weave tail through several stitches to secure.

Make thumb: Insert empty knitting needle into first 8 stitches held on waste yarn. Slip remaining 8 stitches from waste yarn to second needle. Join yarn A at beginning of second needle; place marker to indicate beginning of round. With third needle, knit 8 stitches from second needle; pick up 2 stitches from knit edge above thumb opening; knit 8 stitches from first needle (18 stitches total). With beginning marker in place, rearrange stitches so each needle has 6 stitches. Use fourth needle to knit in rounds until piece measures 2¼″ (5.5cm).

Shape thumb top

Round 1: [Knit 2, knit 2 together] 4 times, knit last 2 stitches together. (12 stitches)

Rounds 2–3: Knit.

Round 4: [Knit 1, knit 2 together] 4 times. (8 stitches)

Round 5: Knit.

Cut yarn, leaving 5″ (12.5cm) tail. Thread tail on tapestry needle, and insert through 8 stitches on needle. Pull yarn gently to close thumb top. Turn mitten inside out, and weave tail through several stitches to secure.

Make second mitten to match.

Felting

Follow felting instructions on page 27. Try mittens on for size several times during felting process.

Be Kind to Your Washing Machine!

Before beginning the felting process, always place knitted pieces in a pillowcase and secure the top. This will prevent yarn fibers from clogging the drain or overloading the lint filter.

Possum Hats

The beauty of these hats is their versatility. Knit them in these three colors; reverse the colors; or choose three entirely different colors. The classic design suits everyone.

Designer: JoAnne Turcotte

Techniques

Binding off—BO (page 14)
Casting on—CO (page 9)
Joining colors (page 21)
Knitting in the round (page 16)
Working with double-pointed
needles—dpn (page 16)

Size

20″ (51cm) in circumference

⊗　⊗　⊗

Gauge

16 stitches/24 rows=4″ (10cm)
in circular stockinette stitch

⊗　⊗　⊗

What You'll Need

Yarn: Soft animal fur and wool blend:
109 yards (100m) each
colors A, B, and C
We used: Cherry Tree Hill Furlana
(80% merino, 20% possum): Ratta
(color A), 1 skein; Natural (color B),
1 skein; Nero (color C), 1 skein
Note: These yarn amounts
will make 2 hats.

Needles: US size 7 (4.5mm) set of
4 double-pointed; US size 9 (5.5mm)
set of 4 double-pointed

Notions: Stitch marker; tapestry needle

Note: The lower edge will curl
forward on its own to form a loose
roll as the work progresses, expos-
ing the purl stitches to the right side
of the work, as shown in photo.

Make the hat

With color A and size 7 needles, loosely cast on 78 stitches. Divide stitches evenly on 3 double-pointed needles (26 stitches on each). Place stitch marker and join into a circle, being careful not to twist stitches. Knit every round until piece measures 1″ (2.5cm) from cast-on edge.

Change to size 9 needles, and continue knitting in rounds until work measures 3½″ (9cm) from cast-on edge. Do not cut color A. Join color B, and work 2 rounds of pattern stitch as follows: [Knit 1 stitch with color B, knit 1 stitch with color A]; repeat to end of round. Cut color A, leaving a 4″ (10cm) yarn tail to weave in later. Using color B only, continue knitting every round until work measures 6″ (15cm) from cast-on edge, ending at marker. Do not cut color B. Join color C, and work 2 rounds of pattern stitch as follows: [Knit 1 stitch with color B, knit 1 stitch with color C]; repeat to end of round. Cut color B. Knit next 2 rounds with color C.

Shape the crown: Continuing with color C, begin decrease rounds as follows:

Round 1: [Knit 11, knit 2 together]; repeat to end of round. (72 stitches)
Round 2: [Knit 10, knit 2 together]; repeat to end of round. (66 stitches)
Round 3: [Knit 9, knit 2 together]; repeat to end of round. (60 stitches)
Round 4: [Knit 8, knit 2 together]; repeat to end of round. (54 stitches)
Round 5: [Knit 7, knit 2 together]; repeat to end of round. (48 stitches)
Round 6: [Knit 6, knit 2 together]; repeat to end of round. (42 stitches)
Round 7: [Knit 5, knit 2 together]; repeat to end of round. (36 stitches)
Round 8: [Knit 4, knit 2 together]; repeat to end of round. (30 stitches)
Round 9: [Knit 3, knit 2 together]; repeat to end of round. (24 stitches)
Round 10: [Knit 2, knit 2 together]; repeat to end of round. (18 stitches)
Round 11: [Knit 1, knit 2 together]; repeat to end of round. (12 stitches)
Round 12: [Knit 2 together]; repeat to end of round. (6 stitches)

Cut yarn, leaving 12″ (30.5cm) tail. Thread tail through tapestry needle, weave through remaining 6 stitches, and pull yarn gently to close top of hat. Weave tail to wrong side and through several stitches to secure. Weave in ends.

Repeat instructions to make second hat, switching color A and color C. The second hat starts with color C, changes to color B, and ends with color A.

Cabled Hat and Scarf

The camel-color merino yarn used in these garments is as comfortable as it is attractive, and the simple cable pattern is a traditional favorite. There's no need to be intimidated by the cables: They're not as hard as they look. Start with the scarf, and move on to the hat.

Designer: Beth Walker O'Brien

Size

Scarf: 6" (15cm) wide,
62" (157.5cm) long
Hat: 22" (56cm) in circumference;
10" (25.5cm) in length from crown
to cast-on; 8½" (21.5cm) with brim
turned upward

Gauge

Scarf: 20 stitches/26 rows=4" (10cm)
in stockinette stitch on size 7 needles
Hat: 20 stitches/28 rows=4" (10cm)
in stockinette stitch on size 8 needles

What You'll Need

Yarn: 592 yards (542m) soft, heavy
worsted weight wool yarn
We used: Karabella Yarns Aurora 8:
#1364 chino, 6 balls

Needles: US size 5 (3.75mm),
US size 7 (4.5mm); US size 6 (4mm)
circular; US size 8 (5mm) circular, each
16" (40cm) long; US size 8 (5mm)
double-pointed, set of 4 or 5

Notions: cable needle; tapestry
needle; stitch marker

Cable abbreviations

C4B: Slip 2 stitches to cable needle and hold to back of work, knit 2 from left-hand needle, knit 2 from cable needle.
C6B: Slip 3 stitches to cable needle and hold to back of work, knit 3 from left-hand needle, knit 3 from cable needle.

Techniques

Binding off—BO (page 14)
Cables (page 19)
Casting on—CO (page 9)
Knit 1 through the back loop—k1tbl (page 18)
Knit 2 together—k2tog (page 19)
Knitting in the round (page 16)
Long tail cast-on (page 10)
Make 1 increase—m1 (page 18)
Ribbing (page 15)
Slip slip knit decrease—ssk (page 19)
Working with double-pointed needles—dpn (page 16)

Cabled Scarf

Make the scarf

With size 5 needles, cast on 47 stitches.

Row 1: (wrong side) With yarn in front, slip 1 stitch purlwise, [purl 1, knit 1] 22 times, purl 2.

Row 2: With yarn in back, slip 1 stitch purlwise, [knit 1, purl 1] 22 times, knit 2.

Row 3: Repeat row 1.

Row 4: Repeat row 2.

Row 5: With yarn in front, slip 1 stitch purlwise, [purl 1, knit 1] 11 times, make 1, [purl 1, knit 1] 11 times, purl 2. (48 stitches)

Row 6: (right side) Change to size 7 needles. With yarn in back, slip 1 stitch purlwise, knit 1, purl 1, knit 1, [purl 3, knit 6, purl 3, knit 2] 2 times, purl 3, knit 6, purl 3, knit 1, purl 1, knit 2.

Row 7 and remaining odd-numbered rows: With yarn in front, slip 1 stitch purlwise, purl 1, knit 1, purl 1, [knit 3, purl 6, knit 3, purl 2] 2 times, knit 3, purl 6, knit 3, purl 1, knit 1, purl 2.

Row 8: Repeat row 6.

Row 10: With yarn in back, slip 1 stitch purlwise, knit 1, purl 1, knit 1, [purl 3, C6B, purl 3, knit 2] 2 times, purl 3, C6B, purl 3, knit 1, purl 1, knit 2.

Row 12: Repeat row 6.

Row 13: Repeat row 7.

Repeat rows 6–13 until scarf measures approximately 61" (155cm) in length. End with row 13.

Row 14: Change to size 5 needles. With yarn in back, slip 1 stitch purlwise, [knit 1, purl 1] 11 times, knit 2 together, purl 1, [knit 1, purl 1] 10 times, knit 2. (47 stitches)

Row 15: (wrong side) With yarn in front, slip 1 stitch purlwise, [purl 1, knit 1] 22 times, purl 2.

Row 16: With yarn in back, slip 1 stitch purlwise, [knit 1, purl 1] 22 times, knit 2.

Row 17: Repeat row 15.

Row 18: Repeat row 16. Bind off in pattern.

Finishing

Weave in all remaining ends to wrong side and weave through several stitches to secure.

Cabled Hat

Fisherman's Rib Pattern
Round 1: *Knit 1 through back loop, purl 1**; repeat from * to ** to end of round.
Round 2: *Knit 1, purl 1**; repeat from * to ** to end of round.

6-Stitch Rope Cable Pattern (crossed every 8 rounds)
Rounds 1–4: Knit 6.
Round 5: Work C6B. (See cable abbreviations, page 148.)
Rounds 6–8: Knit 6.

Make the hat

With size 6 circular needles, cast on 132 stitches. Join stitches into a circle, taking care not to twist stitches. Place stitch marker after last stitch to indicate beginning of round.

Work in Fisherman's Rib pattern for 2½″ (6.5cm). *[Knit 4, knit 2 together] 2 times; [knit 5, knit 2 together] 3 times**. Repeat from * to ** 4 times. (112 stitches)

For Fisherman's Rib pattern to show on the correct side when brim is folded upward, work remainder of hat in opposite direction of brim. To avoid a hole in the work, wrap first stitch of next row as follows: With yarn in front, slip 1 stitch purlwise from left needle to right needle, take yarn to back of work, then return stitch from right needle to left needle. Turn work, and continue in the opposite direction (wrong side of Fisherman's Rib pattern should be facing as you work remainder of hat).

Begin cables: Change to size 8 circular needles and work as follows:
Round 1: [Purl 3, knit 2, purl 3, work round 1 of 6-Stitch Rope Cable pattern] 8 times.

Round 2: [Purl 3, knit 2, purl 3, work round 2 of pattern] 8 times.

Round 3: [Purl 3, knit 2, purl 3, work round 3 of pattern] 8 times.

Round 4: [Purl 3, knit 2, purl 3, work round 4 of pattern] 8 times.

Round 5: [Purl 3, knit 2, purl 3, work round 5 of pattern] 8 times.

Round 6: [Purl 3, knit 2, purl 3, work round 6 of pattern] 8 times.

Round 7: [Purl 3, knit 2, purl 3, work round 7 of pattern] 8 times.

Round 8: [Purl 3, knit 2, purl 3, work round 8 of pattern] 8 times.

Repeat rounds 1–8 for approximately 5½″ (14cm), ending on round 7.

Shape the crown: In the following rounds, C6B is worked on round 6, and C4B is worked on round 14 to accommodate fewer stitches. (Change to double-pointed needles when there are too few stitches to continue on circular needles.)

Round 1: [Purl 2 together, purl 1, knit 2, purl 1, purl 2 together, knit 6] 8 times. (96 stitches)

Rounds 2–4: [Purl 2, knit 2, purl 2, knit 6] 8 times.

Round 5: [Purl 2 together, knit 2, purl 2 together, knit 6] 8 times. (80 stitches)

Round 6: [Purl 1, knit 2, purl 1, C6B] 8 times.

Round 7: [Purl 1, knit 2, purl 1, knit 2, knit 2 together, knit 2] 8 times. (72 stitches)

Round 8: [Purl 1, knit 2, purl 1, knit 5] 8 times.

Round 9: [Purl 1, knit 2, purl 1, knit 1, knit 2 together, knit 2] 8 times. (64 stitches)

Round 10: [Purl 1, knit 2, purl 1, knit 4] 8 times.

Round 11: [Knit 2 together, slip slip knit decrease, knit 4] 8 times. (48 stitches)

Round 12: Knit.

Round 13: [Knit 2 together, knit 4] 8 times. (40 stitches)

Round 14: [Knit 1, C4B] 8 times.

Round 15: Knit 2 together to end of round. (20 stitches)

Round 16: Knit.

Round 17: Knit 2 together to end of round. (10 stitches)

Cut yarn; thread on tapestry needle. Weave yarn tail through remaining 10 stitches on needle, and pull to close top of hat.

Finishing

Weave in loose yarn ends to wrong side of work, and secure.

Take Two

What if you have started a pattern and you're just not happy with it? Do you have to finish what you start? No! Knitting should be relaxing and joyful—and it will be when you've matched your skills to the right project. There are so many great patterns available that you should always be able to knit something that inspires and excites you.

World's Warmest Mittens

The thick, comfy yarn used to knit these mittens will keep hands toasty warm.
And the extra detailing on the cuffs makes them something special!   Designer: Beth Brown-Reinsel

Techniques
Knit 2 together–k2tog (page 19)
Knitting in the round (page 16)
Make 1 increase–m1 (page 18)
Picking up stitches (page 22)
Simple cast-on (page 11)
Working with double-pointed
needles–dpn (page 16)

Size
Adult medium
Circumference at palm: 8″ (20.5cm)
Length from wrist to fingertip, with cuff
turned back: 9¼″ (23.5cm)

Gauge
12 stitches/16 rows=4″ (10cm)
in circular stockinette stitch

What You'll Need
Yarn: About 108 yards (99m) blend of
fibers in bulky weight yarn
We used: Lion Brand Yarn Wool-Ease
Thick and Quick (80% acrylic, 20%
wool): #128 pine, 1 skein

Needles: US size 10 (6mm) set of
4 double-pointed

Notions: Stitch markers; stitch holder;
tapestry needle; a few yards yellow
and red scrap yarn or Lion Brand Yarn
Wool-Ease worsted weight,
1 ball each color

Make the mittens

Cuff: This cuff will be turned back when the mitten is finished, so wrong side will face up as you knit the cuff.

Loosely cast on 22 stitches and divide onto 3 double-pointed needles: 7 stitches on first needle, 8 on second, and 7 on third. Place stitch marker at beginning of first needle to indicate beginning of round.

Round 1: Knit 1 stitch onto needle with marker to hold marker in place; knit to end of round.

Rounds 2–7: Purl.

Body of mitten: This is now the right side of the work. Knit 12 rounds.

Round 13: Knit 10 stitches, place marker, make 1, knit 2 stitches, make 1, place marker, knit 10 stitches. (24 stitches)

Rounds 14–16: Knit.

Round 17: Knit 10 stitches, slip marker, make 1, knit 4 stitches, make 1, make 1, knit 10 stitches. (26 stitches)

Rounds 18–20: Knit.

Round 21: Knit 10 stitches, slip marker, make 1, knit 6 stitches, make 1, slip marker, knit 10 stitches. (28 stitches)

Rounds 22–24: Knit.

There are 8 stitches between markers.

Thumb opening: Knit 10 stitches, remove marker, slip next 8 stitches onto stitch holder, cast on 2 stitches using simple cast-on method, remove second marker, knit 10 stitches. (22 stitches)

Knit even for 12 rounds.

Tip of mitten: Knit 4 stitches, knit 2 together, knit 9 stitches, knit 2 together, knit 5 stitches. (20 stitches)

Next round: Knit.

Next round: [Knit 3 stitches, knit 2 together]; repeat to end of round. (16 stitches)

Next round: Knit.

Next round: [Knit 2 stitches, knit 2 together]; repeat to end of round. (12 stitches)

Knit 2 rounds. Cut yarn, leaving 6″ (15cm) tail. Thread tail on tapestry needle, and draw through all stitches. Pull gently to close top of mitten. Weave tail to wrong side and through several stitches to secure.

Thumb: Slip 8 stitches from stitch holder onto 2 double-pointed needles (4 stitches on each). Join working yarn to inner part of thumb opening, pick up 2 stitches, knit 8 stitches, place marker. (10 stitches)
Next 8 rounds: Knit.
Next round: [Knit 1, knit 2 together] 3 times, knit 1. (7 stitches)
Next round: Knit 1, [knit 2 together] 3 times. (4 stitches)

Cut yarn, leaving 6″ (15cm) tail. Thread tail on tapestry needle, and draw through all stitches. Pull gently to close top of thumb. Weave all tails to wrong side.

Make second mitten to match.

Embroidery: Fold cuff down, and with right side facing, thread tapestry needle with 2 strands yellow yarn. Embroider an open-style line of zig-zags encircling the cuff. Finish off yarn on wrong side of work. Thread needle with single strand red yarn, and work triangles in each space between yellow zig-zag stitches (see photo). Weave in all loose ends to wrong side of work.

Buying Yarn Wisely

- Keep a wish list of things you'd like to make, and then watch for the yarn to go on sale.

- Make a list of the supplies you really need—and don't go yarn shopping without it.

- Don't buy yarn until you have chosen a pattern. If you aren't familiar with the yarn, consider buying just 1 skein to make a swatch—that way you'll know if it's what you had in mind. Even better, look for yarn stores that keep supplies on hand for you to make a swatch before buying.

Resource Directory

Designers

Berroco, Inc.
P.O. Box 367
Uxbridge, MA 01569–0367
www.berroco.com
e-mail: info@berroco.com
(Color-Block Baby Blanket, page 72;
Baby Kimono and Hat, page 78;
Monet Cardigan, page 126)

Beth Brown-Reinsel/
Knitting Traditions
P.O. Box 722
Forest Hill, MD 21050
Phone: (410) 399-9618
www.knittingtraditions.com
e-mail: beth@knittingtraditions.com
(World's Warmest Mittens, page 152)

Lisa Daniels/Big Sky
Studio & Gallery
P.O. Box 566
Lafayette, CA 94549
Phone: (925) 284-1020
Fax: (925) 284-2624
e-mail: bigskys@pacbell.net
(Mixed Fiber Throw, page 32;
Textured Shawl, page 50)

Judy Dercum/La Lana Wools
136–C Paseo Norte
Taos, NM 87571
Phone: (505) 758-9631
Orders: (888) 377-9631
www.lalanawools.com
e-mail: lalana@lalanawools.com
(Curly Striped Pillow, page 45)

Phyllis Fishberg/
The Wool Connection
34 E. Main St.
Avon, CT 06001
Phone: (860) 678-1710
Fax: (860) 677-7039
Orders: (800) 933-9665
www.woolconnection.com
e-mail: wool@tiac.net
(Stripes-and-Solids Sweater, page 92)

Laurie Gonyea/Destination Knits
3419 Morrison St. NW
Washington, DC 20015
www.destinationknits.com
e-mail: destinationknits@yahoo.com
(Double-Knit Slippers, page 134)

Charlene Hatfield/Stitch in Time
722 E. Grand River
Howell, MI 48843
Phone: (517) 546-0769
www.stitchintime.safeshopper.com
e-mail: stitch@ismi.net
(Wavy Rib Socks, page 137)

Darlene Hayes/Hand Jive Knits
Phone: (916) 806-8063
www.handjiveknits.com
e-mail: darlenehayes@
    handjiveknits.com
(Americana Pot Holder, page 36)

Terry Kimbrough/String and Sticks
P.O. Box 114
Romance, AR 72136
Phone: (501) 882-2731
e-mail: tmorris@futura.net
(Honeycomb Stroller Blanket, page 86)

Marilyn King/
Black Water Abbey Yarns
P.O. Box 470688
Aurora, CO 80047–0688
Phone: (720) 320-1003
Fax: (303) 364-3566
www.abbeyyarns.com
e-mail: marilyn@abbeyyarns.com
(Men's Sporty Vest, page 122)

Amy Merritt/Cottage Industry
409 Division St.
Northfield, MN 55057
Phone: (507) 664-3870
www.cottageindustry.net
e-mail: yarnista@cottageindustry.net
(Linen Pullover, page 112)

Needful Yarns & Things Inc.
60 Industrial Pkwy. #233
Cheektowaga, NY 14227
Phone: (866) 800-4700

www.needfulyarnsinc.com
e-mail: info@needfulyarnsinc.com
(Simply Snuggly Turtleneck, page 115)

Beth Walker O'Brien
Phone: (630) 841-3360
www.bethobriendesigns.com
e-mail: beth@bethobriendesigns.com
(Beaded Wedding Purses, page 61;
Watercolor Wrap, page 65; Dream
Baby Hat and Cardigan, page 95;
Ribbon Tank Top, page 109; "It's a
Cinch" Hat, page 140; Cabled Hat
and Scarf, page 148)

Jessica Peterson/Cottage Industry
409 Division St.
Northfield, MN 55057
Phone: (507) 664-3870
www.cottageindustry.net
e-mail: yarnista@cottageindustry.net
(Ruffly Cardigan, page 118)

Lucie Sinkler/CloseKnit, Inc.
622 Grove St.
Evanston, IL 60201
Phone: (847) 328-6760
Fax: (847) 328-0618
e-mail: sinkler@mc.net
(Designer Dishcloths, page 30;
Padded Hanger and Sachet, page 34;
Felted Christmas Stocking, page 39;
Lovely Lace Edging, page 42; Cell
Phone Cozies, page 53; Eyeglass
Case, page 56; Felted Market Bags,
page 58; Baby's Best Booties, page
75; Barnyard Finger Puppets, page
82; Hooded Jacket and Booties,
page 88; Simple Sparkle Scarf,
page 132; Fun Felted Mittens,
page 143)

JoAnne Turcotte
e-mail: jbbturcotte@aol.com
(Possum Hats, page 146)

Sharon Turner/Monkey Suits
542 Lorimer St. #6
Brooklyn, NY 11211

(Monkey Suits, continued)
www.monkeysuits.com
e-mail: sharon@monkeysuits.com
(Trapeze Jacket and Muff, page 99; Striped Overalls, page 104)

Adrienne Welch/Arachne Designs
205 Joy Ave
St. Louis, MO 63119
Phone: (314) 761-7196
Fax: (314) 968-7538
www.arachnedesigns.net
e-mail: adriennewelch@
    arachnedesigns.net
(Elegant Evening Bag, page 68)

Artful Yarns/JCA Inc.
35 Scales Lane
Townsend, MA 01469–1094
Phone: (800) 225-6340
(Lovely Lace Edging, page 42)

Bernat
320 Livingstone Ave. S
Listowel, ON Canada N4W 3H3
www.bernat.com
(Honeycomb Stroller Blanket, page 86)

Berroco, Inc.
P.O. Box 367
Uxbridge, MA 01569–0367
www.berroco.com
e-mail: info@berroco.com
(Color-Block Baby Blanket, page 72; Baby Kimono and Hat, page 78; Hooded Jacket and Booties, page 88; Ribbon Tank Top, page 109; Monet Cardigan, page 126)

Black Water Abbey Yarns
P.O. Box 470688
Aurora, CO 80047–0688
Phone: (720) 320-1003
Fax: (303) 364-3566
www.abbeyyarns.com
e-mail: marilyn@abbeyyarns.com
(Men's Sporty Vest, page 122)

Brown Sheep
100662 County Rd.
Mitchell, NE 69357–9748
Phone: (308) 635-2198

Fax: (308) 635-2143
Orders: (800) 826-9136
(Felted Christmas Stocking, page 39)

Cascade Yarns
P.O. Box 58168
Tukwila, WA 98138
Phone (206) 574-0440
www.cascadeyarns.com
e-mail: sales@cascadeyarns.com
(Americana Pot Holder, page 36; Felted Market Bags, page 58; Barnyard Finger Puppets, page 82; Dream Baby Hat and Cardigan, page 95; Fun Felted Mittens, page 143)

Cherry Tree Hill, Inc.
52 Church St.
Barton, VT 05822
Phone: (802) 525-3311
Fax: (802) 525-3336
Orders: (800) 739-7701
www.cherryyarn.com
e-mail: orders@cherryyarn.com
(Possum Hats, page 146)

Classic Elite Yarns
300 Jackson St.
Lowell, MA 01852
Phone: (978) 453-2837
Fax: (978) 452-3085
Orders: (800) 343-0308
www.classiceliteyarns.com
e-mail: classicelite@aol.com
(Trapeze Jacket and Muff, page 99)

Dale of Norway Inc.
N16 W23390 Stoneridge Dr.,
    Suite A
Waukesha, WI 53188
Phone: (262) 544-1996
Fax: (262) 544-1997
www.daleofnorway.com
e-mail: sales@daleofnorway.com
(Wavy Rib Socks, page 137)

Euroflax Linen
Louet Sales (distributor)
808 Commerce Park Dr.
Ogdensburg, NY 13669
Phone: (613) 925-4502
Fax: (613) 925-1405
www.louet.com

e-mail: info@louet.com
(Linen Pullover, page 112)

Jo Sharp Pty Ltd
ACN 056 596 439
P.O. Box 1018
Fremantle WA 6959 Australia
e-mail: yarn@josharp.com.au
www.josharp.com.au
(Baby's Best Booties, page 75)

Karabella Yarns
1201 Broadway
New York, NY 10001
Phone: (212) 684-2665
Fax: (646) 935-0588
Orders: (800) 550-0898
www.karabellayarns.com
e-mail: info@karabellayarns.com
(Cabled Hat and Scarf, page 148)

Kiparoo Farm Studio
2110 D Pleasant View Rd.
Adamstown, MD 21710
Phone: (301) 874-6348
(Double-Knit Slippers, page 134)

La Lana Wools
136–C Paseo Norte
Taos, NM 87571
Phone: (505) 758-9631
Orders: (877) 377-9631
www.lalanawools.com
e-mail: lalana@lalanawools.com
(Curly Striped Pillow, page 45)

Lily
320 Livingstone Ave. S
Listowel, ON Canada N4W 3H3
www.sugarncream.com
(Designer Dishcloths, page 30)

Lion Brand Yarns
34 W. 15th St.
New York, NY 10011
Phone: (800) 258-YARN (9276)
Fax: (212) 627-8154
www.lionbrandyarn.com
e-mail: customerservice@
    lionbrandyarn.com
(World's Warmest Mittens, page 152)

Lorna's Laces
4229 N. Honore St.

Chicago, IL 60613
Phone: (773) 935-3803
Fax: (773) 935-3804
www.lornaslaces.net
e-mail: yarn@lornaslaces.net
(*Watercolor Wrap, page 65*)

Manos del Uruguay
Design Source (distributor)
P. O. Box 770
Medford, MA 02180
Orders: (888) 566-9970
Fax: (781) 438-6279
(*Ruffly Cardigan, page 118*)

Mountain Color Yarn
P. O. Box 156
Corvallis, MT 59828
Phone: (406) 777-3377
Fax: (406) 777-7313
www.mountaincolors.com
e-mail: info@mountaincolors.com
(*Mixed Fiber Throw, page 32; Textured Shawl, page 50*)

Needful Yarns & Things Inc.
60 Industrial Pkwy. #233
Cheektowaga, NY 14227
Phone: (866) 800-4700
www.needfulyarnsinc.com
e-mail: info@needfulyarnsinc.com
(*Simply Snuggly Turtleneck, page 115*)

Patons
P. O. Box 40
Listowel, ON Canada N4W 3H3
www.patonsyarns.com
(*Padded Hanger and Sachet, page 34*)

Plymouth Yarn Company
P. O. Box 28
Bristol, PA 19007
Phone: (215) 788-0459
Fax: (215) 788-2269
www.plymouthyarn.com
e-mail: pyc@plymouthyarn.com
(*Cell Phone Cozies, page 53; Eyeglass Case, page 56; Elegant Evening Bag, page 68; "It's a Cinch" Hat, page 140*)

Reynolds/JCA Inc.
35 Scales Lane
Townsend, MA 01469–1094

Phone: (978) 597-8794
(*Beaded Wedding Purses, page 61; Stripes-and-Solids Sweater, page 92*)

Takhi Yarns
Stacy Charles, Inc.
8000 Cooper Ave., Building 1
Glendale, NY 11385
Phone: (718) 326-4433
(*Striped Overalls, page 104*)

Trendsetter Yarns
16742 Stagg, #104
Van Nuys, CA 91406
Phone: (818) 780-5497
Orders: (800) 446-2425
e-mail: trndstr@aol.com
(*Simple Sparkle Scarf, page 132*)

Big Sky Studio & Gallery
P. O. Box 566
Lafayette, CA 94549
Phone: (925) 284-1020
Fax: (925) 284-2624
e-mail: bigskys@pacbell.net

CloseKnit, Inc.
622 Grove St.
Evanston, IL 60201
Phone: (847) 328-6760
Fax: (847) 328-0618

Cottage Industry
409 Division St.
Northfield, MN 55057
Phone: (507) 664-3870
www.cottageindustry.net
e-mail: yarnista@cottageindustry.net

Stitch in Time
722 E. Grand River
Howell, MI 48843
Phone: (517) 546-0769
www.stitchintime.safeshopper.com
e-mail: stitch@ismi.net

The Wool Connection
34 E. Main St.
Avon, CT 06001
Phone: (860) 678-1710
Fax: (860) 677-7039
www.woolconnection.com
e-mail: wool@tiac.net

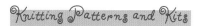

Arachne Designs
205 Joy Ave.
St. Louis, MO 63119
Phone: (314) 761-7196
Fax: (314) 968-7538
www.arachnedesigns.net
e-mail: adriennewelch@
    arachnedesigns.net

Hand Jive Knits
Phone: (916) 806-8063
www.handjiveknits.com
e-mail: darlenehayes@
    handjiveknits.com

Monkey Suits
542 Lorimer St. #6
Brooklyn, NY 11211
www.monkeysuits.com
e-mail: sharon@monkeysuits.com

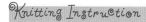

Laurie Gonyea/Destination Knits
3419 Morrison St. NW
Washington, DC 20015
www.destinationknits.com
e-mail: destinationknits@yahoo.com

Beth Walker O'Brien
Phone: (630) 841-3360
www.bethobriendesigns.com
e-mail: beth@bethobriendesigns.com

**Beth Brown Reinsel/
Knitting Traditions**
P. O. Box 722
Forest Hill, MD 21050
Phone: (410) 399-9618
www.knittingtraditions.com
e-mail: beth@knittingtraditions.com

Knitting Accessories

Terry Kimbrough/String and Sticks
P. O. Box 114
Romance, AR 72136
Phone: (501) 882-2731
e-mail: tmorris@futura.net

Knitting Notes

Project ....

Given to ....

Date ....

Yarn used ....

    Brand ....

    Amount ....

    Color ....

Needle size ....

Attach yarn sample here.

Notes ....

....

....

....

Project ....

Given to ....

Date ....

Yarn used ....

    Brand ....

    Amount ....

    Color ....

Needle size ....

Attach yarn sample here.

Notes ....

....

....

....

Project ....

Given to ....

Date ....

Yarn used ....

    Brand ....

    Amount ....

    Color ....

Needle size ....

Attach yarn sample here.

Notes ....

....

....

....

Project ....

Given to ....

Date ....

Yarn used ....

    Brand ....

    Amount ....

    Color ....

Needle size ....

Attach yarn sample here.

Notes ....

....

....

....

Project ....

Given to ....

Date ....

Yarn used

    Brand ....

    Amount ....

    Color ....

Needle size ....

> Attach yarn sample here.

Notes ....

....

....

....

....

Project ....

Given to ....

Date ....

Yarn used

    Brand ....

    Amount ....

    Color ....

Needle size ....

> Attach yarn sample here.

Notes ....

....

....

....

....

Project ....

Given to ....

Date ....

Yarn used

    Brand ....

    Amount ....

    Color ....

Needle size ....

> Attach yarn sample here.

Notes ....

....

....

....

....

Project ....

Given to ....

Date ....

Yarn used

    Brand ....

    Amount ....

    Color ....

Needle size ....

> Attach yarn sample here.

Notes ....

....

....

....

....

Index